The
Mass

sc

The Mass

George Every

GILL and MACMILLAN

Published in 1978 by
Gill and Macmillan Ltd
15/17 Eden Quay
Dublin I
with associated companies in
London and Basingstoke
New York, Melbourne, Delhi,
Johannesburg

Copyright © Webb & Bower Ltd 1978

ISBN 7171 0917 8

A *Webb&Bower* Book
Edited, designed and produced by
Webb & Bower Limited,
Exeter, England

Picture Research by Anne Marie Ehrlich
Design by Vic Giolitto
Printed and bound in Great Britain by
Hazell Watson and Viney Limited,
Aylesbury, Buckinghamshire

Contents

Introduction

This book was written at Oscott, the seminary of the English Catholic archdiocese of Birmingham, where I have been helping with the lecturing and in the library since 1973. But much of the thinking behind it about continuity and change in rituals of worship was done in an Anglican Religious Community, and at their college at Kelham, especially while I was lecturing on liturgy, comparative religion and some Church history from 1950 to 1972. I became a Catholic after that.

It will be clear from the first chapter that I see resemblances between the Mass and sacrifices in other religions, as well as between the Mass and other ritual commemorations of the life and death of Christ. Some of these are not called sacrifices, but where bread and wine are blessed, broken, divided and consumed in memory of the Son of God who died in human flesh for us, the ritual meal can be called sacrificial at least in the wider sense in which Jewish kosher killing and the ritual slaughter of beasts in Islam lead to sacrificial meals, no longer called sacrifices. Such resemblances imply differences. I am not saying that all sacrifices are the same, still less that all are to be reduced to some essential element, some common denominator. But sacrificial rituals do illuminate one another. They ought not to be regarded simply as dramatic or parabolic renderings of what could be said in a more abstract or parabolic way in a sermon. They speak a language of their own.

Six of the eleven chapters of this book are concerned with the history of the Roman Mass in the narrower sense, from its first emergence as a Latin rite to the recent changes that have transformed the Tridentine Missal of 1570 into the *Missale Romanum* of 1970, in Latin and in translations. Four are concerned with antecedents in pre-Christian and early Christian rituals of worship, and only one with alternatives to the Mass proposed in the crisis of the Reformation, although some of these appear again as part of the background to the recent changes. My object is to put these in their context first in the long history of Latin liturgy, and then in the circumstances of the present day.

The text of the Roman Mass, so far as the important invariable parts are concerned, took shape at an early stage before there was any controversy about the real presence of the body and blood of Christ under the forms of bread and wine or the place of sacrifice in the Mass. But the ways in which Mass was offered in abbeys, cathedrals, parish churches and chantry chapels in towns and villages all over Western Europe, varied very widely indeed. Uniformity in texts and ceremonies was partly a consequence of the invention of printing, which made it possible to circulate texts with detailed directions, but the extent of detail had much to do with the controversies of the Reformation. These made ecclesiastical authorities aware of abuses, and fearful of scandal. Movements seeking further reforms by a return to sources common to East and West, and respected by Protestants, began soon afterwards, but the presence of an elaborate machinery for regulating rites put limits on the possibilities of experiment.

These did not apply outside the institutional bounds of the Catholic Church, and so

Anglicans and Protestants engaged in like enquiries into primitive liturgy under Catholic influences were able to devise new liturgies of their own. My own involvement with such liturgical experiments as an Anglican has made me aware of their role in liturgical change in the Catholic Church. It may be that in places I have exaggerated this, and have seen a direct influence where I should only have seen an instance of two groups of people with like concerns engaged on a similar problem. I do not mean to imply that the problems are the same. There is more in common on the level of meaning between the Roman Mass and Eastern liturgies, celebrated in substantially the same forms by Eastern Catholics in communion with Rome and by other Eastern Churches in schism with Rome and with them, than there is between any of these traditional liturgies and those composed after the Reformation in Churches separated from Rome for reasons that have to do, among other things, with the meaning of the Mass. Nevertheless all these Anglican and Protestant rites are derived from the Roman Mass and cannot be understood without it. In this way they are more like it than they are like the Eastern liturgies. As some of the pictures in this book show, they have something in common with present Catholic practice. It does not follow that Catholics, in reforming the same rites, are moving in the same direction. Rather they are learning from the successes and failures of Anglicans and Protestants how to reach a level of common participation by the whole people in the whole ritual hitherto unknown.

G.E.

I Original Rituals

We all engage in lamentation and incantation, in gestures and sounds that express woe and entreaty or content and a sense of satisfaction, before we make any use of articulate words. A mother's relations with her baby are established by rituals of repetition in which familiar movements and murmurs convey assurances from one to the other that all is well. We observe similar exchanges between animals, not only in the care of the young but in courtship displays, in billing and cooing, and in signals of agitation and alarm. These make sense to other species, including ourselves. Sheep and sheepdogs communicate with one another by styles of movement. A dog responds to signals from his master. As signs and gestures can convey a meaning where no common language is spoken, so in all communication with minds of a different order symbols that convey their own sense prevail over sights and sounds that belong to the particular vocabulary of a special group.

Muslim prayers in the open, alone in the evening.

8

This principle applies not only to men and animals, but to all attempts to communicate with spirits, gods or demons. The good Muslim who takes a room in Birmingham or Chicago and signs on for a new job there, is first of all concerned to know the direction of Mecca. He may not be able to unroll his mat at the proper times at his place of work, as he will at home, but he will speak under his breath the words of a traditional form of incantation. This is as much a ritual as the beginning and end of a Quaker meeting, where there may be silence all the time, but silence in a posture of prayer, or as the hubbub of prayer and praise at a pentecostal gathering. On the other hand there are forms of worship where ritual is residuary, in that the primary purpose of the gathering is to convey theological and moral ideas from the minister to the members or from the members to one another.

It is impossible to reduce the Mass to this level. No doubt the Christian eucharist has been celebrated by those who regard it as a parable to be interpreted, as a kind of acted sermon, but no sermon can exhaust the meaning of the mystery com- memorated in the Mass. Where the life and death of Jesus are seen simply as a supreme example of self-sacrificing service, the ritual commemoration of his death and burial has only an historical connection with the subject of this book. The difference in kind between the Mass and a memorial service for a hero or prophet

Muslims at prayer before a mosque.

has nothing to do with the controversies of the Reformation. Zwingli indeed regarded the Protestant Lord's Supper as a commemoration of the sacrifice of Christ, related to his sacrifice on the cross as a memorial, as the sacrifices of the Old Testament were types and shadows, symbolic representations of the cross. But while Luther, Calvin and Zwingli refused to allow that the Mass could properly be called a sacrifice, they all believed that the sacrifice of Christ is made present in the holy communion, Luther and Calvin (in rather different ways) that his body and blood is received, Zwingli that those who make their communion are symbolically reminded of Christ's gracious work. All were concerned with positive connections between the sacrifices of the Old Testament, the death and resurrection of Christ, and the communion of Christians in his risen life. All agreed with their Catholic opponents that the death of Christ is called a sacrifice in relation to other sacrifices in the Old Testament, and that the Mass can be called sacrificial, a feast upon a sacrifice, only in relation to Christ's death on the cross.

In the Bible, an authority for all of them, sacrifice is taken for granted. The story of Cain and Abel is not a tale of the origins of sacrifice. The compiler of this part of the book of Genesis assumes that the sacrifices of beasts and of first-fruits of the earth are established customs for the original human beings. He sees these rites in terms of an age when omens of success or failure could be read in the entrails of the victim and in the sizzling of the cooked meal in the pot; but the place of the story in the biblical narrative shows that sacrifice is regarded as human, not specifically Semitic, older than the disposition of peoples recorded after the Flood, before Abraham and Noah, in the first age of humanity.

Those who look for the origins of sacrifice in the art of the Ice Age can therefore claim to be in a tradition common to Israel and Christendom. Man was a hunter and food-gatherer before he was a herdsman and a farmer. Hunting is still a ritual, not only among the bushmen in the Kalahari Desert, but for riders to hounds, who assemble at a meet and proceed to the chase after regular rituals have been performed, culminating in further ceremonies at the kill. The early history of this kind of ritual has been illuminated in the present century by the discovery of drawings, paintings and small pieces of sculpture in a number of caves in the south of France and the north of Spain.

These can be dated with safety before 10,000 B.C., in an age when a thick sheet of ground ice covered the British Isles, the North Sea, and northern and central Europe. The animals mainly portrayed, bison, mammoth, ox, horse, bear and reindeer, are otherwise known to have roamed over tundra like that of Siberia in France, Italy and Spain. The duration of the Great Ice Age is uncertain; it may have lasted ten thousand years or four hundred centuries. On either reckoning the length of the period in which the drawings and paintings were made is longer than the whole history of agriculture. Concerning the relative dating of periods within this time the record of the rocks gives us accurate geological information. The art of the caves belongs to the age when the human species took its present form.

Those who founded the civilizations of the Middle East, of India and China, and of the two Americas, were descended from hunters. We know a good deal about their hunting neighbours, not only on the borders of China and Mongolia.

Primitive types of agricultural societies can be observed in Arizona and New Mexico among the Pueblo Indians. There and in some other places in America it is possible to speak of a transition between the hunter and the peasant. But in these instances it would be unwise to assume that there has been no penetration of ideas from a superior civilization. In such places as East Africa and Arabia herdsmen and farmers have influenced hunters through the whole of history. And where we can be reasonably sure that there has been little or no infiltration from developed civilizations, it is unwise to assume that primitive cultures never change. Some of the Australian aborigines have made changes in their rites of initiation since they were first observed and recorded. Some of them may be end-products of a long line of development, like their complicated rules of kinship.

What is distinctive about the art of the Ice Age is that it can be regarded as first-hand evidence, however difficult it is to interpret, of attitudes to the earth and animals before any cattle, sheep or horses were tamed, or fields tilled. These lie behind the religious reverence of African tribes for their cattle, and the attitudes of Orthodox Hindus to the sacred cow. We have now discovered enough caves of the palaeolithic period, before any agriculture at all, to make some cautious generalizations. It is as if we had found a number of ruined churches of various periods, with no liturgical books and few liturgical instruments, but with much of the wall decoration more or less intact. This enables us to make sense of a number of small objects found at different times on other sites of the same period, incised weapons and tools, statuettes and amulets, and occasional sketched or painted stones, which may be regarded as sketches for some of the paintings and drawings found in the caves.

Jan van Eyck's portrayal of 'The Lamb slain from the foundation of the world' in Revelation 13:8 is also related to the scene described in chapter 4 of the same book. It was made for St. John's, Ghent, where it still is, in 1426.

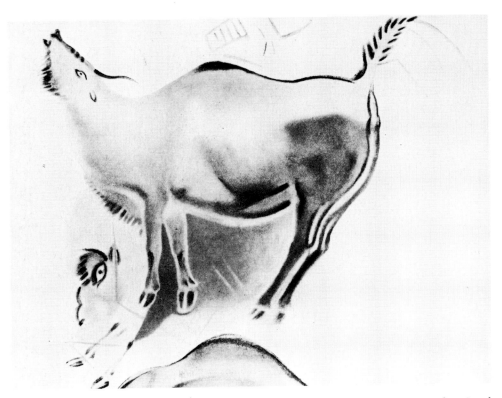

This is a bison painted in the cave of Altamira, near Santander in the north of Spain.

These, especially the paintings, show an extraordinary mastery of animal movement, and command of the means to represent it. The nature of the animals represented, including for instance the reindeer and the woolly mammoth, as well as bear, bison, horses and elephants, makes it quite certain that they belong to the Ice Age. Moreover, they are so placed that they cannot be seen without great difficulty, at the end of long, winding passages, far away from any natural light, and they are often drawn and painted in palimpsest, as we say of manuscripts, on top of one another. Those who made them by the light of dim, flickering lamps, of which traces are sometimes found, must have known how to find the appointed place for them, nearly always at a considerable distance from the surface of the ground, but they cannot have seen more than one at a time.

Of one thing we can be certain, that the paintings were not made to be admired by spectators for their decorative effect. Again a comparison with church buildings is apposite. In many churches the decoration of the roof has only become visible from the floor through the modern use of electric light. The total effect of a series of cave paintings, which is often very impressive, can never have been seen by men before Altamira, in northern Spain, was explored in 1879, and then Sautuola's discoveries were received with considerable scepticism. Nearly all the systematic exploration has been done in the twentieth century, much of it under the direction of the Abbé Henri Breuil. Most of the drawings and paintings are of beasts in action. Some have signs painted on them in the form of arrows or of a figure that may be intended to represent a trap. Bison are carved in the act of sexual intercourse, and a

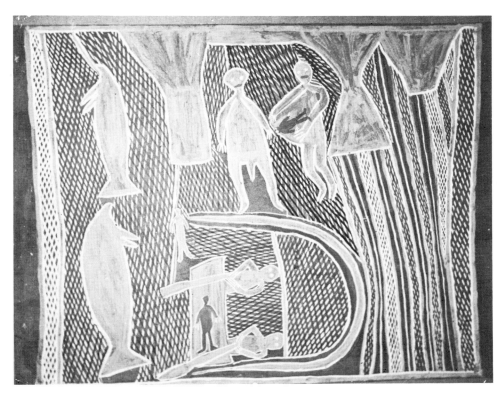

Australian aboriginal painting on bark praying for the safe delivery of a child, in terms of a voyage from a submarine underworld.

bear with his head cut off and a bear's skull between his paws, presumably the last of a whole series of bears' heads struck off the model in what may be called a ritual rehearsal. It could be contended that this was part of a ritual of initiation for younger hunters, and that all the drawings and paintings preserved in the caves served a practical purpose as tests of ability to move in the dark toward a determined goal, and there to record understanding of animal movement, and of the right place for a mortal wound. Experienced hunters who came after them would be able to see enough to judge their work. Yet this explanation is not sufficient to account for the elaborate concealment of all this art in the heart of the earth.

At the time when the art of the Ice Age was first investigated, the magical explanation was favoured by many anthropologists. This is based on the observed fact that many people, not only in primitive societies, but also in advanced civilizations, have a strong impulse to enact their desires in representations, visual, musical and literary, and some belief that these may effect what they signify. If for instance they are made in anticipation of what is expected, of the autumn rains, of the return of spring, or of the birth of a baby or of a calf, the magic may appear to succeed, and it may be repeated on a like occasion. There is no doubt that this does happen. It is another matter to explain religion by the failure of magic, and to hold that gods and spirits are devised to explain the situation when women weep, but there is no rain, when they water their window-boxes, but the spring is still delayed, and rock a doll in a cradle, but the expected child is not conceived or is miscarried.

This curious theory of the priority of magic to religion has very little evidence to

13

support it. It has been influential as providing the basis for Sir James Frazer's *The Golden Bough,* a work of immense industry and erudition, largely derived from missionary sources, devoted to the study of superstition, and of the origins of the great religions. Frazer believed that human beings everywhere passed through three stages of development, from magic through religion to science, and that as the progress of intelligence revealed the limitations of magic, spiritual beings were invented to account for the failure of spells. In this view the original god is the one who fails, and thereby shows that without his aid the magic will not succeed. When he in his turn is found to be bogus, a path is paved for the rise of experimental science.

This atheistic myth of religious origins had an extraordinary vogue at the beginning of this century, as the palaeolithic art of the caves was coming to light. It was commonly compared with paintings made on the surface of the rocks by Australian aborigines. Some of these paintings are said to represent desirable fruits, but others depict human faces, with eyes and noses but no mouths. These must be kept in good condition, or the rain will not fall. If they had mouths, it would rain all the time. This is magic, intended to have an automatic effect, but on weather spirits. A number of small human faces found in the Trois-Frères, a cave in the central Pyrenees, were interpreted by the Abbé Breuil as "the souls of animals . . . or elementary spirits who guide their actions". In the same cave are three composite figures, including one with a bison's head and hoofs, playing a musical instrument. It is hard to interpret this in terms of pure magic, with no spiritual agent other than the artist, and this also seems to be true of much, though not of all, Australian art.

Magic and religion are certainly not independent of one another, but magic should be regarded as a means of exercising spiritual influence on others, which may be directed at a particular person or spirit or to the world in general, spiritual and material. In all religions prayers may continue as spells when their original address has become vague or forgotten. So pagan rites survive among Christians and Catholic rites among Protestants. We throw salt over our shoulder to meet the demands of the demon who made us spill it, and say "bally" and "bloody" for "by Our Lady".

Laurens van der Post in *The Lost World of the Kalahari* tells of a visit with some bushmen to a remote sanctuary where "the master spirit of each animal, bird, insect and plant that had ever been created" was believed to be with "the master spirit of all spirits". The pictures seen at the place included some "of animals which, like the charging rhinoceros, no longer existed in this part of the world". Van der Post goes on to describe what he saw where once had been a cave, before a landslip broke it open:

> In the focus of the painting, scarlet against the gold of the stone, was an enormous eland bull standing sideways, his massive body charged with masculine power and his noble head looking as if he had only at this moment been disturbed in his grazing. He was painted as only a Bushman, who had a deep identification with the eland, could have painted him. Moreover it seems that he had been painted before the Bushman's serenity was threatened, for the look of calm and trustful inquiry on the eland's face was complete.

The little Lady of Laussel in the Dordogne, carrying a bison's horn. She is to be compared with smaller statuettes of the same Aurignacian period, and with the goddess figures of Malta, the Cyclades and the Middle East.

This reads like a novel, and indeed Colonel van der Post insists that it is one, and that therefore anthropological criticism is irrelevant. But at least it is a sympathetic interpretation of the attitude of bushmen to their painting by one who all his life has known them well. If such places as Modderpoort in the Orange Free State, where many such paintings are found, were regarded by bushmen as shrines where they could communicate with animals and their tutelary spirits, the same was probably true of Altamira, Trois-Frères, Lascaux and other caves in France and Spain. Several of these contain sketches of composite human and animal figures or of human beings dressed in animal skins. In only one, at Laussel, a small figure of a great lady is carved in low relief on the wall. She is pregnant, and bears a bison's horn. She is of the very earliest period of cave art, the Aurignacian, and resembles tiny statuettes of maternal figures that have been found in sites of the same period all over Europe and western Asia. These have a family resemblance to figures of the mother goddess in the first age of agriculture. It is not unlikely that the little lady of Laussel, the other Aurignacian statuettes, and the mother goddess of the Middle East stand for the same mother earth whose subterranean sanctuaries were at Laussel, Altamira and Lascaux, and afterward at Eleusis, in Cyprus, and at Babylon, in sanctuaries of Demeter, Aphrodite and Ishtar.

The address of the pictures is speculative, but their content is sure. In Ice Age art they imply wonder at the strength and vitality of the great beasts, and a desire to participate in this through killing and eating, but not at the expense of the herd as a whole, which must be preserved in order that some may sometimes be killed. Where the choice of the victim is determined, as it must generally have been, on its place in the herd itself, the first steps are taken on the long road that leads from what we would classify as game preservation to what we would call the domestication of animals. But this is a very long road, and it is best understood if we think of it not in economic terms, but in terms of relationships that still persist between African tribes and their cattle. In one of the pyramid texts the saying is found: "Well tended are men, the cattle of god". In the time of the first pharaohs it was well understood that men look after cattle. They get some profit from them, but they see them as a source of strength rather than as a supply of meat.

In a normal herd a chief bull would be in command, who will let no one else serve his cows. In time a bull-calf will challenge and dethrone him, but so long as he reigns he is the head of the herd and the symbol of strength and fertility for the whole community. In time he may come to recognize that human hunters can be trusted to protect his cows and their calves, not only from marauders but from rivals. So he may come to acquiesce in the killing of bull-calves, and even to welcome it, until he outlasts his strength and in the eyes of the hunt is ripe for sacrifice, his successor for inauguration.

Freud came to believe that the same had happened to human beings, and his prestige as a psychoanalyst has given to his anthropological fantasies an authority that still persists. In a human group it is impossible to imagine a single man with power to defend a number of women and their children from marauders and rivals and to do all the hunting for them. Animals are not killed instead of rebellious children, although children no doubt were willingly identified with slaughtered calves and lambs, killed and eaten for the welfare of the whole tribe and herd.

The idea that the beast is a substitute for a human victim, a ram caught in a thicket for a chief's son, is one that naturally arises and indeed becomes appropriate to the situation, as soon as the herd becomes a possession of the human group. But in the age of transition between hunting and herding the tribe belongs to the herd, not the herd to the tribe. The tribal god was portrayed in the form of a great beast or of a monster combining the features of man and beast. The so-called "sorcerer" in the cave at Trois-Frères has been naturalistically interpreted as a dancer dressed in skins

This figure painted in and on the cleft of a rock in the cave of Les Trois Frères, Ariége, in the south of France close to the Pyrenees, is commonly called 'The Sorcerer'. It is, however, more likely to represent a being of a different order, in whose body the suppliant can take refuge.

16

with a stag's antlers. He is painted in and around a cleft in the rock, large enough for a man to lie in, and it is more likely that he represents a god, in whose body the initiate took refuge by lying down or standing in the cleft of the rock, within him. The cult of the horned god persisted in Europe, and coloured the medieval image of the devil. Often he serves for a figure of fertility, but he is never represented with a consort of the same shape. Rather he is the servant of the goddess, who is human from the very first. She is the earth, the mother of all, impregnated from the heavens. She is not sacrificed as the beasts are, but she receives what sinks into the ground and is buried there. Libations are poured to her as a way of acknowledging that we all return to her, that our blood, like the wine, the blood of the grape, and the blood of the slaughtered beasts, returns to the earth.

Christians and Pagan Sacrifices

The ritual slaughter of beasts extends to religions that have limited sacrifice in a proper sense to particular times and places, or have abolished the sacrifice of animals. Jewish Kosher killing and the ritual killing of beasts in Islam are sacrificial in a wide sense. Christians at the time when the New Testament was written were frequently faced with a choice between meat killed in a temple, and so in their terms sacrificed to an idol, and no meat at all, when kosher meat was not available, or Jewish butchers kept it for Orthodox customers. St. Paul allowed that they could eat sacrificed meat if they took no part in the ceremonies, but this ruling (in I Cor. 10: 25–9) was difficult to interpret, and others might have been more strict.

Some sixty years later, around A.D. 112, the younger Pliny was anxious about the decline of sacrificial offerings in Bithynian temples. It is clear from his correspondence with the Emperor Trajan that while the Christians were being blamed, the decline was out of proportion to their numbers. They had begun to create a market for unsacrificed meat. This was no doubt cheap, but a source of alarm to the municipal authorities, not only because the temples depended on sacrifices for their supplies, but also because ritual slaughter was publicly controlled. The risk of diseased meat would be increased if cattle could be killed in any street.

It is in this context, where most meat meals were sacrificial, that the Mass came to be called a sacrifice. It is never so called in so many words in the New Testament, although St. Paul (in I Cor. 10:21) compares "the table of the Lord" with "the table of demons", clearly referring to a pagan sacrificial meal. It is a sacrifice, "your sacrifice", in Chapter 14 of the *Didache,* "the Teaching of the Apostles", which could be contemporary with parts of the New Testament, but this is a reason for thinking that this little book was written in a Gentile, not in a Jewish community. Jews would not naturally use the word sacrifice of a ritual meal without any comment or explanation. To Gentiles any ritual meal was sacrificial. The word "sacrifice" was used without hesitation, and without definition, where Christians were surrounded with a variety of sacrifices.

In the early Roman Empire spirits of the dead and spirits of the air were an accepted part of the world picture. Nearly everyone was agreed that to invoke them is dangerous, unless they have already taken the initiative and laid hold of a prophet or prophetess, a shaman or some other sort of possessed person, or of the

Australian aborigines dance in celebration of the creative powers.

This cast of a figure found in Malta is a link between the Aurignacian mother-figures and Middle Eastern mother-goddesses.

priest or priestess of a shrine where offerings are made in sacrifice on behalf of a community, of a clan or family, or of some voluntary society. Christians believed that it would be wrong for them to take part in such traditional rituals, however they were authorized, because among the spirits invoked and present on such occasions some were probably sinister and all might well be hostile to them. If their bodily presence could not be avoided, they would refrain from any kind of participation. They believed, in the words of St. Paul (Rom. 1:20–25), that God indeed shows himself in the world, that "ever since the creation of the world his invisible nature, namely, his eternal power and divinity, has been clearly perceived in the things that have been made . . . Men did not honour him as God or give thanks to him . . . Claiming to be wise, they became fools, and exchanged the glory of the immortal God for images resembling mortal man or birds or animals or reptiles . . . They changed the truth of God for a lie and worshipped and served the creature rather than the Creator . . ."

Among the creatures served were "lights in the firmament of the heavens", given "for signs and seasons, days and years" in Genesis 1:14. The place of the noonday sun among the stars in the heavens was a matter of intense interest to those who needed a more accurate calendar of seasons for sowing and planting, sailing, harrowing and reaping, than the succession of the moon's phases week by week and month by month could provide. This was sufficient to calculate gestation, for calves, foals and children, but not for the precise date of the spring and autumn equinox, for midsummer day or the winter solstice, for the right time to expect rain and to sow seed. For this the sun and moon, the planets and the fixed stars, were relevant in their several ways and in their mutual relations. They were all read as signs, and they came to be conceived as having influences of their own, within the framework of the common order, as part of the host of heaven.

Neither Jews nor Christians denied that the positions of the sun and moon, the planets and the stars, can tell us where we are in the calendar, and that the same knowledge may tell us something about our probable moods and the right and wrong days for our enterprises, if it is correctly related to the hour and place of our birth. But they denied that the influence of the heavenly bodies was inexorable. Like everything else, it is subject to divine control and may be changed by the operations of grace in response to prayer. The same might be said of similar conclusions that could be drawn from other forms of augury. As the migrations of birds are signs of summer and winter, and seagulls flying inland of storms, so a number of magpies on our right and left may tell us what kind of day it will be for us, but not inevitably. The majority of early Christians came from families and communities accustomed to consult the gods by such means, through astrological predictions, through the flight of birds, or through auspices seen in a sacrifice, through auguries in the condition of a sacrificed victim, in lines in the liver and in other entrails. Christians rejected all of these, the last with especial emphasis, since they refused to take part in the ritual of sacrifice for the sake of enquiring of a god or of the gods. But their objections to taking horoscopes were fundamentally the same, that such enquiries expose us to the influence of deceitful spirits. Indian and African Christians today have to make the same decisions. They do so with less difficulty because the science of our day is on their side. But neither now nor at that time is the decision simply a negative one. Christians have other ways of enquiring of God.

The Christian Mystery Religion

In the next chapter we shall be considering the sacrifice of Christ on the cross and in the Mass in relation to its peculiar background in the religion of Israel. Christianity can also be considered as one of a class of mystery religions that spread round the Mediterranean before and soon after the rise of the Roman Empire. The Orphic brotherhoods, the Eleusinian mysteries, the cult of the Egyptian Isis, and Mithraism, have all been compared with primitive Christianity, not only by social and psychological investigators seeking to analyse the origins of the Christian religion, but by the early Christians themselves, who provide a great deal of our information about them. The basic resemblance between mystery religions is that they were practised by societies of initiates. They received converts. Even the Eleusinian mysteries, which were originally a part of the agricultural religion of Attica, won their prestige through the many students who came to study at Athens and were initiated in their formative years. They saw them as part of their spiritual education. So these and other mystery religions transformed rituals originally connected with the place of a person in an established society, with fertility, generation and growth, birth, copulation and death in Attica and Egypt, into rites of regeneration preparing the initiate for life in a new dimension, as a liberated man of Greek education, or as one who had gone down into the darkness and returned with some of the wisdom of the Egyptians. As Eleusis stood to Athens and the temples of Isis to Egypt, so the Mithraeum stood to the old religion of Persia, and so it could be contended that the Synagogue and the Church stood to the ancient religion of Israel.

A good deal of work on the relation of the mysteries to their origins was done at the beginning of this century, notably by Miss Jane Harrison in her *Prolegomena to the Study of Greek Religion,* published in Cambridge in 1903. When this book was written the study of Ice Age art had scarcely begun, and the explorations of Sir Arthur Evans in Minoan Crete were still at an early stage. Nevertheless the book stands up in the light of later developments much better than *The Golden Bough.* However it suffers from the author's inevitable failure to recognize pre-agricultural, hunting rituals, where the animals are the gods who impart life and strength to men. In myths relating to the Orphic mysteries where the god Dionysus is himself killed and eaten she suspected a concealed cannibalism: "The suspicion is inevitable that behind the primitive Cretan rites of bull-tearing and bull-eating there lay an orgy still more hideous, the sacrifice of a human child" (p. 489). "A sacrificial bull, or possibly a child, was torn to pieces and his flesh eaten. Who tore him to pieces? In actual fact his worshippers, but the myth-making mind always clamours for divine precedent. . . . In a sense the worshipper believes the sacrificial bull to be divine, but, brought face to face with the notion of the dismemberment of a god, he recoils" (pp. 491–2). Miss Harrison cited from Aelian a story that the people of Tenedos used to sacrifice a new-born calf. "The man who struck it with

Opposite: Sacrifice to Dionysus on a vase in the British Museum.

the axe is pelted with stones in the holy rite and escapes to the sea". She comments: "The conclusion can scarcely be avoided that here we have a ritual remembrance of a time when a child really was sacrificed. . . . That the calf was regarded as a child is clear; the line between human and merely animal is to primitive man as shifting shadow." But so is the line between animal and god. The calf was a symbol of the god, as in Egypt and in the northern part of the kingdom of Israel.

As new relations between man and beast develop in societies where the cattle are no longer lords, but beasts of burden, the god as well as the goddess is bound to become human or superhuman. In a moment of crisis a fatted calf, or a lamb of a year old, is no longer a sufficient means of communication with the divine host. Miss Harrison did not see that in the original Cretan rite a bull, ritually slain in a bull-fight, regularly represented on cups from Cnossos, was in normal circumstances an adequate figure of male divinity, and a bull-calf the traditional object of sacrifice. The Orphics, who had come to stand for a spiritualized idea of the regenerative power of the saviour god, had need to think of the calf as an unsatisfactory substitute for a better representative of the new life. They therefore told the story of how the Titans slew and ate the young Dionysus, with important consequences for themselves and for mankind.

Confusion was introduced into the subject by a Byzantine novelist, who wrote an exciting tale of a civil servant who forsook the court for the wilderness of Sinai. There he was obsessed with anxiety lest the bedouin should kidnap his son and tear him to pieces, as they did "a white camel, otherwise flawless, when the supply of boys was lacking. . . . With their knives some cut off a small piece of hide with the hair upon it, others hack at any chance piece of flesh they can get. Others go on to the entrails and inward and leave no scrap of the flesh uneaten. . . . They do not even refrain from the bones and marrow, but by patience and perseverance overcome the toughness of the resistance."

This was taken for autobiography by Professor W. Robertson Smith of Aberdeen, who was deceived by its inclusion among the ascetic works of St. Nilus of Ancyrá[*], a man of less literary culture but of more mature spirituality, living in the period ascribed by the novelist to his hero. Robertson Smith was so impressed that he made the story a foundation for a theory of the origins of sacrifice in *The Religion of the Semites*, a book whose first edition was published in 1889. By that time he was in serious trouble with the Church of Scotland. He had left Aberdeen and taken refuge in Cambridge, where Miss Harrison and others accepted him as an authority on primitive religion.

The novelist may have had reason to believe that bedouin sometimes ate their camels raw, but it is unlikely that his account of their feast depends on the testimony of anyone who had ever exposed himself to the considerable physical and spiritual risks involved. The part of the story on which Robertson Smith built most is the tale that Arabs prefer to sacrifice "boys in the flower of their age and of special beauty". This is likely to be a tale told to the children to warn them against wandering into the desert.

The Orphics and other votaries of mystery religions were idealists. They looked for a full, perfect and sufficient sacrifice. They wanted more than assurance of a full

[*]In *Patrologia Graeco-Latina* 79 (Paris 1865) cols. 611–14.

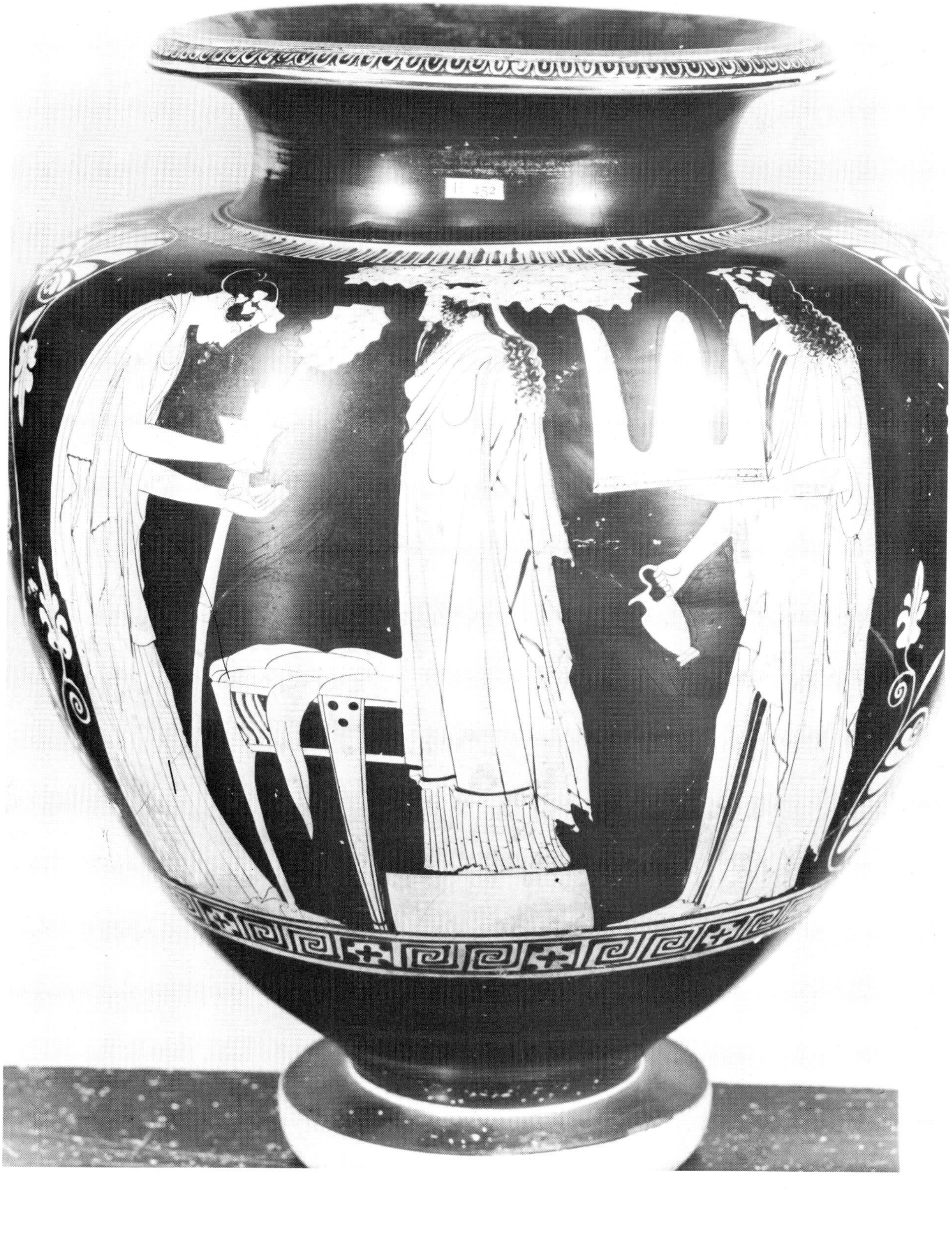
E 452

meal, of good crops next year and a safe passage through it for themselves and their wives and children. They wanted new life, here and beyond the grave, an inspiration from divine wisdom. They saw their sacrifice in terms of eating and drinking the flesh and blood of the young Dionysus, of receiving inspiration from his charismatic wine.

The Christians could meet these demands, and more. They gave communion in the sacrifice of a victim who was himself the second Adam, the archetypal, original and representative man, and in him the Word of God from heaven, the Eternal Son of an Almighty all-Father. The presence of a god in the sacrificed flesh was an old idea that had become difficult to believe as ideas of the divine grew more remote from our fleshly condition. It now came back again in a form that was concrete and tangible, connected with the living memory of a man who could be presented not only as the Son of God but on the human level as an impressive sage whose sayings were memorable, whose risen presence in the Holy Spirit was a source of inspiration, not only ecstatic, but moral and intellectual. On all these counts the Christian mystery met the same demands as the other mysteries, and others on which contemporary philosophy was wont to insist. But there was a price to pay. Those who were initiated into the orthodox Christianity of the Great Church were obliged to resign, not only from other mysteries, but from any office or occupation that involved them in any form of active participation in any cult, including those of the gods of their family and trade, and of the empire and genius of Rome.

The Christian mystery was therefore universally recognized as a subversive religion. It was not like the other mysteries, an optional extra, a private cult to be practised in addition to civil, imperial and family religion, but a new way of life for the inhabited universe. If it were not extirpated, other religions would fade away. No doubt there were some who thought that the Christian repudiation of all other religions but their own was one way of escaping the obligations of society and of the family. This was probably confirmed by the daring of Christians who disappeared into the wilderness and were with the wild beasts. On the other hand it was qualified by observation of the actual behavior of Christians to one another, to their children, and to those who joined them. Many of the widows who became Christians had been forsaken by their own and their husband's families; concubines were admitted on condition that they were loyal to one man, and reared their babies. A new way of life was coming into being that could persist in a falling world and therefore could become the basis for another civilization.

Many who regard themselves as adherents of the Christian way of life and of the philosophy of Christ will be offended by the presentation of Christianity as a mystery religion. They are right to insist that from the very first it was more than that. The other aspect will be seen most clearly in relation to Israel in the next chapter; but it was as a mystery religion in the back streets of cities, and not among the Jews, that Christianity made progress and took shape. The terms common to all the mysteries are older than any of them. They represent a return to pre-agricultural religion in an urbanized society of a kind that recurs in our own post-agricultural age. The crumbling of cultures brings us back to the purely human, to our elementary need to communicate in a life that is older and stronger than our own.

II Sacrifice in the Bible

Distinctive Ideas of the Old Testament

No one who has any knowledge of the Jewish people will wish to deny that they are in a special way peculiar. Those Jews who no longer believe that they are the chosen heirs of the promises of God or practise any part of the Jewish law, are still very much aware of their identity with Israel's past, and with the present sufferings of Israelites in the Soviet Union and in the Muslim world, their past sufferings at the hands of the czars, the Nazis, and in the Middle Ages. But not everything in Israel is distinctive. The Jews have something in common with other peoples who have been their neighbours and kinsmen, and then their adversaries in the present and in the remote past. Too much emphasis on the distinctive ideas of the Old Testament can distort the picture as much as denial that anything distinctive is there.

In the matter of sacrifice, the sacrificial rituals prescribed in the Old Testament have parallels in other religions. Most of them refer to ritual meals in which the worshippers as well as the priests took part. In the religion of Israel, as in other religions practised around the Mediterranean, the whole burnt offering, totally consumed by fire into smoke and ashes, was important but exceptional. What made the aspect of offering specially important in sacrificial meals was the necessity of taking the victim to the appointed sanctuary, or in the case of the Passover at any rate to the immediate neighbourhood of Jerusalem. This distinction between a sacrifice at Jerusalem and a ritual meal, with blood poured out beforehand, in any ordinary Jewish home, is a development whose history can be traced through the books of the Old Testament, from the days when the patriarchs sacrificed on their camping sites, upon altars erected for the purpose, through times when "the high places were not taken away" and the people of Israel sacrificed "on every high hill and under every green tree". However, our present awareness of historical sequence in this is relatively recent. Commentators before the nineteenth century regarded the law of the single, central sanctuary as going back to the time of Moses. Deviations from this had taken place by divine command under special circumstances, but the cults in the high places were heretical, probably pagan.

Jewish and Christian commentators were alike convinced that Jeroboam, the son of Nebat, "made Israel to sin" by setting up golden calves at Bethel and Dan to represent the God of Israel "who brought you up out of the land of Egypt", as recorded in I Kings (12:28). A fragment from a story favourable to this conviction has survived in Exodus (32:24), where Aaron tells how the figure of a golden bull was formed out of gold provided by the people, and came out of the fire. Those who beheld in the bull the symbol of divine power included Jehu, who was anointed king at the command of the prophet Elisha (in II Kings 9) to overthrow the "whoredoms" of the Tyrian queen, Jezebel, and the worship of the Phoenician Baal. Jehu "did not turn aside from the sins of Jeroboam the son of Nebat . . . the

The Mass of St. Giles in the National Gallery, the work of an unknown painter who was in Paris around 1500. The Church is St. Denis. The king is intended to be Charlemagne, whose sins are shown on a scroll by the angel to the saint, with a promise of pardon if he will repent, and of pardon to others who seek the prayers of St. Giles. The historical St. Giles was of another time and place, but his relics and story were diffused widely.

27

Frontispiece to Leviticus in the Bible from the library of the Arsenal, now in the Bibliothèque Nationale in Paris. The scenes include the worship of the golden calf (centre), Moses breaking the tables of the Law (right), and the disasters of Korah and his company, who swing censers without effect, and are swallowed up. (Numbers 16)

Opposite: Melchizedek sacrifices bread and wine at his meeting with Abraham in Genesis 12, represented in a mosaic in St. Maria Maggiore at Rome.

golden calves that were in Bethel, and in Dan'', according to II Kings (10:30). Yet the Lord and the prophets of the Lord, the disciples of Elijah and Elisha, are represented as approving of his revolution, and of the purging of alien influences from the commercial cities of the coast. Those who regarded the bulls at Dan and Bethel as thrones for the Lord himself looked for signs of his will in the victims sacrificed there, in calves, kids and lambs. While there are no indications in the Old Testament of any such elaborate methods of augury through the study of entrails as developed in other religions, sacrifice is associated with the sacred lot given by Urim and Thummim in I Samuel (14:41) and elsewhere. There are other signs that priests were expected to interpret the will of God in some prophetic way associated with ritual, to give judgement in cases of perplexity.

This does not mean that there was no important difference between Jewish and Gentile ideas of God until the law of a single sanctuary was definitely established and all religious imagery eliminated that could be used in an idolatrous way. As we shall see, the perils of idolatry are still present in a different form in Israel after the exile, and in Catholic and Protestant Christianity, but it is a mistake to suppose that idols are always alien, importations from another religion.

Christian attitudes to sacrifices in the Old Testament have passed through three distinct phases. In the early centuries, when the Bible meant the Old Testament, the whole of it was read as a series of promises, prefigurations and prophecies of Christ. From this point of view the ceremonial law was less interesting than the psalms and the prophets, major and minor. Christians read the books of Genesis and Exodus for the story of Creation and the Fall, of Adam and Eve, the serpent and the promised restoration, of Cain and Abel, Noah and the Flood, of the captivity of Joseph in Egypt and then of his whole family and nation, of the miraculous rescue of Israel by signs and wonders, the plagues, the crossing of the Red Sea, the thunders on Sinai. The details of Mosaic legislation were not so interesting. A number of particular sacrifices, especially at the Passover and the Day of Atonement, had been related to the life and death of Christ by the writers of the New Testament, especially by St. Paul and by the writer to the Hebrews, who was often, but not always, supposed to be the same person. These had their share of attention, but they were probably pictured in terms of familiar sacrifices in the religions around them, religions that many Christians had been brought up to practise.

The Latin Christian world became really interested in the last part of the book of Exodus, and in Leviticus very much later, when pagan sacrifices had disappeared or been driven underground. Yet an increasing number of priest-monks in wealthy sanctuaries read the Old Testament in the night office and began to identify themselves with the servants of the Lord in the temple. The first long commentary on the Book of Leviticus was written by Rabanus Maurus in the second half of the ninth century, at a time when controversy was beginning about the meaning of the real presence and of sacrifice in the eucharist.

St. Thomas Aquinas held that offering sacrifice is a duty incumbent on all men according to natural law, but that "the particular way in which sacrifices are offered is determined by human or divine institution". "Adam, Isaac, and other just men offered such sacrifices to God as were fitting for the times when they lived, for in ancient times . . . original sin was remitted through offering sacrifices" (*Summa Theologica*, 2a2ae. 85,1). He cites St. Augustine (85,3) as saying: "A true sacrifice is any work done in order that we may cleave to God in spiritual union." "The very fact that we wish to be spiritually united with God shows reverence for God. Consequently, the act of any virtue assumes the character of sacrifice if it is performed in order to cling to God in spiritual union." He says later (in 85,4) that "sacrifice is twofold; the first and more important is internal sacrifice, and to this all are held since all are held to offer a devout mind to God. The other is external sacrifice. . . . Here the obligation differs for those under the New or Old Law and those who are not. The first are bound to offer set forms of sacrifice according to the precepts of the law. The others, however, were held to perform certain external actions in God's honor, not in the manner prescribed by the law, but in accord with the custom of the people". St. Thomas recognises that "in every age and among all nations sacrifices have always been offered" (85,1). Even under the new law "there are other sacrifices which anyone can offer God on his own behalf". But he has already said that . . .

> a sacrifice in the proper sense of the word means that something is done to the thing offered to God, for example, when animals were killed and burned, and when bread is blessed, broken, and eaten. . . . Oblation, on the other hand, is the direct offering of something to God, even if nothing is done to it; thus we speak of offering money or bread at the altar and nothing is done to them. Hence every sacrifice is an oblation, but not every oblation is a sacrifice. First fruits are oblations because they are offered to God, but they are not sacrifices because they are not made sacred. Tithes, properly speaking, are neither a sacrifice nor an oblation because they are not offered immediately to God but to the ministers of divine worship (85,3).

In another place (1a2ae. 102,3) St. Thomas applies these traditional principles to particular sacrifices in the Old Testament. He regards them all as figures of our own sacrifice of ourselves, our souls and bodies to God, and at the same time as figures of the sacrifice of Christ. "We offer a calf, when we overcome the pride of the flesh; a lamb, when we curb our irrational impulses; a goat when we conquer lust; a turtle dove, when we preserve chastity." He adds to this quotation from the *glossa ordinaria*, the standard commentary on the Bible in the Middle Ages: "And the dove clearly signifies charity and simplicity of heart." He quotes again from the same gloss: "Christ is offered in the calf to signify the power of the cross; in the lamb to signify innocence; in the ram his dominion; in the goat, the likeness of sinful flesh." He gives priority to the whole burnt offering, considered as a sacrifice for the sins of the nation. His comments on the peace-offering, on ritual meals where the worshippers have a share, are revealing. He notes that as a general rule neither the blood nor the fat were eaten by anyone, and says that one reason for this was to avoid idolatry, citing from Deuteronomy (32:38), "Who ate the fat of their sacrifices, and drank the wine of their drink offering", with reference to the gods of Canaan. He says of the Egyptians that "they worshipped sheep; they venerated goats, since demons appeared in their shape; and oxen they used for agriculture, which they held sacred". He seems to think that they did *not* sacrifice these sacred animals, but he has some idea of the role of communion in the victim in sacrifices to idols. He had some insight into the motives of pagan religion, though his historical knowledge was limited.

As attention came to be concentrated on some particular sacrifices noted in the New Testament as types of the sacrifice of Christ, these and others were increasingly seen in terms of Christ himself going up to Jerusalem for the final passover, for his offering of himself at the Last Supper and in the Garden of Gethsemane, his scourging and his bleeding to death on the cross. St. Thomas says elsewhere (3a. 48,3) that "on the part of those who put Christ to death, the passion was a crime; on the part of Christ, who suffered out of love, it was a sacrifice. And that is why Christ himself is said to have offered this sacrifice, and not those who slew him".

The scapegoat driven into the wilderness, naturalistically depicted by the English Victorian painter, Holman Hunt.

We shall see the accents in this shifting in preaching and prayer from the twelfth to the sixteenth century at a later stage in this book. Our business here is to notice the effect on Christian understanding of the Levitical sacrifices. This continued in and after the Reformation. I quote from a small book, *Religion at Home*, published by an Evangelical lady at Islington in North London in 1844 – "a series of conversations between a mother and her daughter on important Scripture subjects". The comments cited are on the goats offered in Leviticus 16.

I purpose drawing from the literal account, recorded by the Jewish lawgiver, some spiritual views, to which those external observances seem to lead the Christian mind. And I may notice, in the first place, that the goat is not a creature possessed of any very amiable properties; on the contrary, that animal is found, in general, to display a degree of perverseness, not seen in many others of the brute kind. For this reason, it may appear strange, that the Lamb of God should be prefigured by a creature so utterly opposed to his meek and lowly character. But, do you not recollect that it is written, that God sent "his Son in the likeness of sinful flesh"? May not the obstinate nature of the goat, then, fitly represent the rugged, unyielding disposition of those, whose sins the lovely Redeemer bore? Again, the goat, though commonly considered an unclean creature, was classed among the clean beasts in the law of Moses. From this we may learn, that Jesus Christ, though reputed as a sinner among men, and dealt with as such by God, was, nevertheless, free from the least taint of contamination.

To Annie, who usefully asks, "But, why were two goats appointed? or, if two were necessary, why was one slain and the other preserved alive?" her mother replies:

Oh, my love, the design of this command is perfectly clear. Both are to be contemplated as types of the great propitiatory. The first goat may signify the complete satisfaction which Christ made to Divine justice by the offering up of himself: and the second goat may show the blessed result of his propitiatory sacrifice. . . . Whilst considering these practices, we seem to hear a voice saying "Christ being come an high-priest of good things to come, neither by the blood of goats and calves, but by his own blood, he entered in once into the holy place, having obtained eternal redemption for us."

This last quotation is from Hebrews (9:12), in the authorized version. The lady certainly supposed that her theology was scriptural, but we can see that it is also in a direct line of succession from the *glossa ordinaria*, put together about a thousand years before.

In 1844 this tradition was still common to Catholics and orthodox Protestants, but it was already beginning to be superseded by a new approach in some respects nearer to that of the early Christians, in that the central message of the Old Testament was seen not in the law, but in the prophets. The priestly code began to be regarded as a survival of primitive religion, purged from the worst errors of idolatry and superstition by prophetic influences, but hardened into another institutional system after the return of the Jews from exile in Babylon. The teaching

The use of figures from the Old Testament, as symbols of spiritual pilgrimage through the earthly life, by Johann Heinrich Roos, a painter at the Court of the Palatinate from 1664–1685, in a portrait of himself and his wife.

of Jesus was a renewal of the prophetic protest against institutions, continued by St. Paul, but transformed into an institutional system in what was called early Catholicism. The Reformation was another prophetic protest against further developments, later fossilized into Protestant scholasticism, and a new Reformation was needed to recover what was truly distinctive in the teaching of the Bible – an ethical monotheism.

There was an important element of truth to history in this view. Valuable discoveries were made, which few would now seek to contradict, about the historical development of Jewish and Christian institutions, but they were made in a perspective not only distinctively Protestant, but coloured by the new philosophy that had arisen in Germany since Kant and Hegel. Early Christians were aware of discrepancies between the chronology of the Greek, Hebrew and Samaritan versions of the Old Testament, and the practice of spiritual interpretation gave them a certain freedom in reconciling differences between biblical and other sources. When such matters were reconsidered in the light of new information about ancient and oriental history and other continents, Protestants were apprehensive that any questioning of the authority of the Hebrew text as established in the Synagogue, as they thought, before or just after the time of Christ, might be used by Catholics to exalt the authority of the Church. Catholics on the other hand were afraid that any new interpretation of the Bible would undermine the authority of tradition, and at the same time make it more difficult to build a bridge whereby Lutherans and Anglicans might return to Catholic unity.

The spiritual interpretation of the Scriptures suffered casualties in these controversies. It has never died; in preaching, meditation and prayer it is still alive, and in our own day it is receiving a new lease of life, not only in the renewed study of mystical interpretation by such Catholic exegetes as Cardinal Daniélou and Père Henri de Lubac, but at the grass roots in the charismatic movement, both Catholic and Protestant. The Anglican pioneers of biblical criticism, S. T. Coleridge and his disciples, Hort, Westcott and F. D. Maurice, were much concerned with mystical interpretation in the Greek Fathers; but the pace in controversy was set by German Protestants, whose interest in the history of the Church was of a much more negative kind. Catholics, and conservative Anglicans, were naturally in sympathy with conservative Protestants in their objections to the assured results of higher criticism. Those who saw the Bible as inspired literature with a purpose other than the exact record of events as they happened, found it difficult to contribute to the debate, not only in the Roman Catholic Church, where considerations of pastoral prudence determined the attitude of ecclesiastical authority to the publication of essays in controversy, but in the Church of England, where they found themselves assailed on both sides for evading the issue: "Is the Bible true? Was the Lord Jesus telling a lie when he spoke of David as the author of a psalm, and compared himself to Jonah in the belly of the whale?"

One God, One Sanctuary

The question at issue is whether Jewish monotheism is to be regarded as a product of prophetic and moral insight, in some way parallel to the religious philosophies of

China, India and Greece, or as a peculiar development of the national religion, in this respect more like Hinduism than Buddhism or Islam. Much turns on the origin of the first two of the "ten words" recorded twice, in Exodus (20:3–4) and Deuteronomy (5:7–8):

1. "You shall have no other gods before my face." It is not said that no other gods exist.

2. "You shall not make for yourself a carved image, or any likeness of anything in heaven above, or in the earth beneath, or in the waters under the earth." "For yourself" is important, as well as what follows: "You shall not bow down to them or serve them."

The matter considered in the first chapter of this book is relevant. What is forbidden is the making of representations of heavenly or infernal powers, as well as of hills and lakes, plants and animals. The theme is continued in the next commandment against using the name of God for our own ends. Representations of powerful beings are used to obtain, by allegiance to them, some kind of influence or control over elements in this world. The Lord's name can be used in this way, but so to use it is vain. Grounds for this are given next: ". . . for in six days the Lord made heaven and earth, the sea and all that is in them". The six days refer to the story of creation, not necessarily in the form that now stands in Genesis 1. The days, here and

This mosaic at St. Pudenziana in Rome has suffered a good deal from repair and restoration, but there is no doubt that the original design was intended to represent the rock of Golgotha, the Rotunda of the Holy Sepulchre, and other buildings round them as they were in the fourth century. The symbols of the four Evangelists in the background, as man, lion, ox and eagle, are here represented visually for the first time.

there, are not a measure of time, but an order of succession. They mean that the elements of light and darkness, of heaven and earth and the underworld, are all derived from the same source of power and holiness, with land and sea, life and inert matter, fish and birds, beasts and reptiles by sea and land.

This ultimate ground is identified with the Lord God of Israel. Other peoples have come to perceive a unity in the cosmos, a common source and also a conflict of elements within it, a host of heaven in harmonious order, and demonic powers in rebellion against the original order of creation. The Israelites were singular in holding that God and his angels were in action in their own history to deliver them from this rebellion, and from their own temptation to join in the rebellion of powers who have fallen into sin. These powers have deceived man by promising him possession of this world over which they have tried to establish their rule in defiance of God, and so they have enslaved men to themselves through the uncontrolled desires of men and women.

It has been thought that the ban on images of living creatures was originally propaganda against the calves of Bethel and Dan. An objection to this theory is that the prophetic movement in northern Israel does not seem to have begun with opposition to these images, but with objections to the cult of the Tyrian Baal. The prophet Hosea, who does object to idolatrous practices in the sanctuary at Bethel, seems to be protesting in the first place against silver models of the golden calf, made and kissed, treasured and used. The calf itself has been misused for the same idolatrous purposes, and will be taken away into captivity. But Jeroboam the son of Nebat, who first made the calves, may have modelled them on the twelve oxen under the molten sea in the temple at Jerusalem, as described in I Kings (7:25). These were supports for a symbolic image of the throne of God over the firmament of heaven, like the ark where God might be conceived as "sitting between the cherubim". The ark was older than the temple. It had belonged to the Tabernacle. Attempts had been made to use it as a talisman on the field of battle, but these had led to disaster. In ancient history the presence of the ark had indeed brought victory, but only when it was taken by God's command to the River Jordan, and round the walls of Jericho, and God himself showed his power in action by staying the waters of Jordan, as he had driven away the waters of the Red Sea, to give his people the victory.

We need not read this story as literal history in our modern sense of the word, a record of events that can be established by impartial testimony. The point is that the Israelites believed that their ancestors were slaves delivered from captivity in Egypt by a series of acts of God, no doubt articulated and elaborated in the telling, as miracles always are. But what makes a miracle is not any breach in the natural order. The Israelites and their adversaries – Babylonians, Canaanites and Egyptians – alike believed that superhuman beings were in action all around them, in wind and wave, flood and storm. What made the Jews distinctive was their belief that their own God was present in their disasters as well as in their triumphs. They regarded their tribulations as his judgements, as part of his saving work. They could not use him for their own purposes, but he could and would use their enemies for his, even against them.

The scourging of Christ, by the Protestant painter, Cranach.

The law of the one sanctuary was a consequence of this. The Jews came to believe that they had been constantly tempted to treat their God as the Gentiles treated the spirits "on every high hill and under every green tree". As a result of this their attitude to sacrifices changed. These ceased to be occasions of enquiry into the will of God, and became more like other offerings in God's honour. Whole burnt offerings were still changed into fire and smoke going up into heaven. The blood of the victim was poured out into the ground, not only in the temple yard, but in butcher's yards at home. But these offerings became simply part of their obedience to the written law. For Jews of the Dispersion, who seldom went up to Jerusalem, the sacrificial ritual had become part of a book, reverently read in the synagogue, and interpreted as a series of signs of their election and purpose. Such signs were no

37

longer seen in the sacrifices themselves, duly performed according to ritual prescriptions as long as the temple lasted, and then simply remembered. Judaism could go on without a temple.

One Sacrifice

In the forty years before the war that led to the fall of Jerusalem and the destruction of the temple there in A.D. 69–70 the Christian movement sprang up and won many adherents in Galilee, and some in Judea and Jerusalem. It continued to grow among the Jews after the execution of the original leader by crucifixion, and won more adherents in the Jewish Dispersion, outside Palestine. There it spread even more rapidly among Gentiles who had been attracted to the worship of the one God in some of the Jewish synagogues, until by the end of the first century A.D. it had become predominantly a Gentile movement.

There is much dispute today about the content of the original teaching of Jesus, developed by his disciples in the light of what they regarded as communion with him in his risen life, in the course of their own experience of growth and transformation, while the new religion was taking shape. Yet the record of the last days of Jesus' life in and around Jerusalem is remarkably complete in all the four gospels and it must have a basis in historical fact.

This much can be said without fear of contradiction, that Jesus of Nazareth came to Jerusalem for the Feast of the Passover, that he received an enthusiastic welcome from many of the pilgrims thronging the streets of the city, and that he came into conflict with the authorities, not only with the priests through his attacks on the traffic in the courts of the temple, but with the rabbis, themselves critical of the priests, through his scathing comments on the traditional interpretation of the law. They combined to denounce him to the Roman governor as a threat to law and order in the city and the country. The gospels represent Pilate as unwilling to accept the accusation, and it is possible that their Christian authors were concerned to attenuate the share of the Roman authorities in the death of Jesus, and to put all the blame on the Jews who rejected the Christian claims, because they wanted to distinguish the Christian movement from Jewish unrest in Palestine before and after the great revolt against Rome, and to rebut the accusation that they worshipped a crucified criminal, condemned to death according to law. St. Luke (23:1–16) represents the priests and scribes as accusing Jesus of a claim to kingship which neither Pilate nor Herod would take seriously, and Pilate as yielding to a clamour for his death, engineered by a coalition of parties generally opposed to one another.

What is perfectly clear is that some of his followers already believed Jesus to be the Messiah, not another prophet, like St. John the Baptist, but the fulfilment of prophecy. They held that God had again intervened decisively in history, as he did at the exodus from Egypt and the crossing of the Red Sea, commemorated at the Passover. The priests trembled for their position and for the safety of the sanctuary. Rabbis of all parties, including Pharisees, who were generally sympathetic to Messianic hopes of a resurrection before very long, nonetheless agreed with the priests that this outsider was a blasphemer. Pilate may or may not have believed that the political peril was serious. Herod almost certainly did not, and treated it as a

Imago triumphalis Tituli vivificæ Crucis D.N.Iesu Christi, qualis hodiè Romæ apud Cistercien. intra Basilicam S. Crucis in Ierusalem, seu intra Capellam Sacrar.^{um} Reliquiarum conspicitur, cuius Tituli Veritatem, Atq. Inventionem Bulla Alex.Pap. VI. Dat.Romæ Die 29. Iulij 1496. plenissimè Testatur; Characteres autem infabrè tunc temporis sculptos, ut vides, vetus tas paulatim læsit, sed Hebraicos magis.

joke. But Pilate and Herod between them, or Herod's Idumaean soldiers, followed by the soldiers of the Roman garrison who took part in the crucifixion, gave to the proceedings the character of a ritual action, when they dressed the victim in a purple robe, crowned him with thorns, and saluted him as King of the Jews. There is no reason to doubt that Pilate himself was responsible for the inscription mounted on the cross, in Hebrew, Greek and Latin, "Jesus of Nazareth, King of the Jews".

Pilate's knowledge of Messianic hopes was that of a sardonic observer of the many varieties of oriental religion and superstition. But he would be familiar with the idea of a sacred king, sacrificed in the spring to turn away the wrath of the powers of heaven, of the old year slain to bring in the new in peace and prosperity. He would also be familiar with the idea of the new year emerging out of the tomb in victory at the conclusion of a new year festival in the spring. To put a guard over the tomb of a sacrificed king would be appropriate to such an occasion, after a ceremony performed in mockery. Nor is it altogether improbable that the guard slept the sleep of the drunken.

Arnold Toynbee, in his elaborate *Study of History*, annexed two very long appendices to Volume VI, published in 1939, dealing for the most part with "correspondences between the story of Jesus and the stories of certain Hellenic saviours". He reached the conclusion that a number of accounts of historical

This print was made in the eighteenth century of a board found in a box over the chancel arch of Santa Croce 'in Jerusalem' in Rome in 1496, and since venerated there as part of the title, in Hebrew, Greek and Latin, over the cross of Christ. Little Hebrew is there, but the Greek and Latin letters of *Nazarenus* are in the Hebrew order, from right to left.

39

The crosses discovered at Jerusalem, and the true cross of Christ identified by a miracle of healing. From a series of frescoes by Piero della Francesca at Arezzo.

characters, including Jesus of Nazareth, had been assimilated to that form of the legend of Hercules in which he goes down into hell to capture Cerberus, and to rescue Alcestis, the wife of King Admetus, and through this to an older myth where the spirit of the year was killed in winter and came back in the spring. The interest of these parallels is that they show the kind of reception that might be given to any account of a saint or saviour who was put to death at the Passover, or at any other feast at the turn of the year. He would still be regarded as a sacrifice for the sins of his folk, even if he had not been crowned with thorns, or worn the purple robe. It was enough to be saluted as King of the Jews, and put to death for his claim to the holy throne.

The New and the Old Testament

The problem for the early Christians was not to prove that Christ's death was a sacrifice. He had given himself, and his offering had been accepted, transfigured, as they believed, in his resurrection and ascension into heaven. He was the Son of Man, representative of all mankind. They believed that they had been made partakers of his life. St. Paul wrote in his letter to the Romans (6:3–4): "Do you not know that all of us who have been baptized into Christ Jesus were baptized into his death? We were therefore buried with him by baptism into death, so that as Christ was raised from the dead by the glory of the Father, we too might walk in newness of life."

The problem was to show how this was "according to the Scriptures", in conformity with the Old Testament. Jewish objections to this were valid as far as

Opposite: A painting by Bellini, of Christ going down into Hell. The naked dead who are with him are not allowed to enter hell or heaven, but like Dante's unfortunates, who never were alive, kept out of both.

40

they went. What the Jews inherit is the prophetic and passionate protest against making any images of God, because all such images are unsatisfactory and can be used for the ends of ambition and rebellion. It is evidently true that they rejected Jesus in obedience to that prohibition, because he did claim to be more than a prophet, to be God in action, whatever may have been the terms in which he himself made this claim. The Christian understanding of the situation developed outside Judaism, because there was no room for it in the old Israel. Yet the Old Testament continued to be part of the Christian inheritance, not only because Jesus and the apostles, including St. Paul, were Jews, but because the Christian conception of God's action in history as Jesus conceived in the coming of the Kingdom of God is specifically Jewish. It may have analogies elsewhere, as in Persia, but it cannot be transformed into material for a philosophical system. The Bible resists every effort to make a metaphysical theory out of it, or even a biblical theology. The danger for Christians in attempts to do this is that they may be tempted to read the New Testament in terms of the Old, instead of reading the Old Testament as preparation for the New.

III Institution of the Eucharist

The Last Supper

The earliest account of the Last Supper is in St. Paul's first letter to the Corinthians (11:23–7). In the gospels St. Matthew follows St. Mark, while St. Luke is nearer to St. Paul, and St. John has no direct reference to the institution of the eucharist then and there. As historical documents St. Paul's letters are very unlike Cicero's, collected for their style, or the younger Pliny's, assembled as models for civil

The Seder meal at Passover as represented in a Jewish manuscript of the fourteenth century.

מעל הבית ונגב ביתן שאומרית יהודה

'Before the Passover', in a Hebrew illustrated manuscript of the fourteenth century.

servants learning the art of administration. It seems that they may have been taken out of cupboards where the order of the pages, and the dates of the letters could have been confused. They are more like charters, or vestments found in a grave, or other archaeological evidence from what has been left about and found by accident. The gospels on the other hand are like lives of the saints, or Plutarch's lives of illustrious men, or Xenophon's *Memorabilia* of Socrates, or in the case of St. John, the dialogues of Plato where Socrates is commemorated. Those who believe in the inspiration of the Scriptures will hold that Christ and the Holy Spirit were involved in the composition of the gospels and of St. Paul's letters, not only in the way in which Socrates may be said to have been involved in the dialogues of Plato. But this does not remove the disparity between letters and lives. In a culture where history was regarded as a branch of rhetorical literature, all histories, not only biographies of illustrious persons, are larded with speeches. Thucydides, Livy and Sallust are full of them. No doubt the speeches often contain characteristic turns of phrase, as well as parables and other stories authentically remembered, but they were never meant to be read as verbatim reports.

The point is important because St. Paul in writing "I received from the Lord what I delivered to you" (I Cor. 11:23) is sometimes represented as claiming a special revelation of the circumstances in which the eucharist was instituted. He was writing in a crisis in the Corinthian Church, and no doubt he prayed about it, but he meant to repeat what he had told them before, and nothing in his letter prevents us from thinking that he refers in the first place to traditions that he had received from other disciples at Jerusalem and Antioch. This serves to explain the substantial identity of his account with the one in St. Mark (14:22–4). Both say "that the Lord Jesus on the night when he was betrayed took bread, and when he had given thanks, he broke it" and gave it to them. In St. Mark "he took a cup, and when he had given thanks he gave it to them, and they all drank of it". The words spoken are "Take; this is my body" and "This is my blood of the covenant, which is poured out for many". St. Paul expands them into "my body for you" and "the new covenant in my blood", and adds in both cases the command to "Do this in remembrance of me". He also comments to the Corinthians, "As often as you eat this bread and drink the cup, you proclaim the Lord's death until he comes."

We know something of the context of St. Paul's retelling of the story, and of his comment, in his desire to insist that anyone who "eats the bread or drinks the cup of the Lord . . . without discerning the body, eats and drinks judgment upon himself". He will incur not only spiritual but physical danger: "That is why many of you are weak and ill, and some have died." He is certainly insisting on the same kind of real presence in the eucharist that is implied in the sixth chapter of St. John's Gospel: "Unless you eat the flesh of the Son of Man and drink his blood, you have not life in you . . . For my flesh is food indeed and my blood is drink indeed. He who eats my flesh and drinks my blood lives in me and I in him" (6:53–6). We know from another and earlier passage in the same letter that St. Paul regards "the cup of blessing which we bless" as "a participation in the blood of Christ", and "the bread which we break" as "a participation in the body of Christ" (10:16). He compares the eucharist not only with pagan sacrifices, with "the table of demons", but with the practice of Israel in sacrifices of praise. Indeed a particular reference may reasonably be assumed to the sacrificial inauguration of the old covenant between Israel and their God in Exodus 24, where "peace offerings of oxen" are made by "young men of the people of Israel". "And Moses took half of the blood and put it in basins, and half of the blood he poured on the altar." He then read the book of the covenant to the people, who promised to obey. "And Moses took the blood and sprinkled it on to the people and said, 'The blood of the covenant which the Lord has made with you in accordance with all the words of this book.' Then Moses and Aaron, Nadab, Abihu and seventy elders" went up to eat and drink in the presence of God, "and there was under his feet as it were a pavement of sapphire stone, like the very heaven for clearness" (Exodus 24:6–11).

The Seder meal at Passover in Yemen, or among those from Yemen now in Israel.

This very vivid story would be familiar, not only to St. Paul but to the apostles at the Last Supper. It seems most likely that the reference was already present and understood in what Jesus himself said there. The account of this in St. Paul, St. Mark and St. Matthew – who follows St. Mark – is a myth in the sense of a tale told to explain the origin of a rite by telling the story of its foundation. St. Luke tells the same tale rather differently, rather as if he were aware of the difficulty of setting the story in the context of the Passover meal. In Chapter 22 (14–21), he puts the cup first at verse 17, with the saying: "Take this, and divide it among yourselves; for I tell you that henceforth I will not drink of the fruit of the vine until the Kingdom of God comes." The bread follows, with "This is my body", and in most manuscripts "given for you", and the command to "do this in remembrance" as in St. Paul. These continue with a second cup, "the new covenant in my blood, poured out for you", but without the command to continue the rite. But in a valuable Greek manuscript, the Codex Bezae, and in the Old Latin version before St. Jerome, the second cup is omitted, with everything after "This is my body". The Gospel of St. John has no account of the institution at all in a long account of the Last Supper, with discourses on what could be eucharistic themes and the story of Christ washing his disciples' feet. Yet as we have seen in other places the author clearly refers to the eucharist, and in terms that are like St. Paul's. He does, however, imply that the Passover began on the day of the crucifixion. This discrepancy between St. John and the other gospels has been discussed for centuries. It may not be in itself very serious, since it is quite possible that some devout people ate the Passover meal before the proper day, as good Catholics used to make their Easter communion on Holy Saturday or even on Good Friday. The real difficulty which has been illuminated and then concealed in these discussions is the discrepancy between the meaning of the eucharist for St. Paul, St. John and the whole Christian Church before the fifteenth century, and the words put into the mouth of Christ by St. Paul and St. Mark, if we think of them as spoken to the disciples at the Last Supper. Both of them make him say of the bread "This is my body", and of the cup "This is my blood", while he was alive and sitting with them, in the normal condition of a man. On the face of it the words cry out to be taken metaphorically, but St. Matthew repeats them, and St. Luke the first if not the second phrase, which in his gospel may be an interpolation. One way of explaining this is to insist that the metaphorical sense of Christ's presence in the eucharist is the original one, and that St. Paul misunderstood it or has been misunderstood. But such an explanation gives rise to intractable difficulties, which cannot be solved by attempts to conflate metaphorical and real senses. A better way is to consider what words could have been used and remembered.

We are told by the linguists that "the copula is not expressed" in Aramaic. That means that there is no ordinary word for "is". What Jesus said at the Last Supper was "this my flesh" and "this my blood" or "this new covenant in my blood", but as he spoke he gave bread and a cup "for you" to his disciples. Whatever he said or meant about "do this in my remembrance", the disciples did it and came to understand it as participation in a new covenant between God and man through the blood of Christ, shed next day on the cross.

St. Paul could have been the first to compare "the table of the Lord" with "the table of demons", the sacrifice of Christ with the sacrifices of Gentiles who partake of saving victims. He was not the first to see the eucharist in a sacrificial setting, as instituted by Christ at the Passover meal before his death in Passover time. But this was not seen as the first eucharistic celebration. We are nearer to this at Emmaus, in St. Luke (24:30–1), on the first Easter evening when Christ, sitting at table with two of his disciples after a long walk from Jerusalem, "took bread, and blessed and broke and gave it to them". He disappeared, leaving himself in the form of bread, "known to them in the breaking of bread", held by them in their trembling hands. But even this is not, strictly speaking, a celebration of the Christian eucharist, which began as disciples deliberately "did this in remembrance" of him, no doubt calling him into table fellowship in accordance with his promise to be with them "where two or three are gathered in my name", and finding to their surprise a more and more intense sense of the presence of his risen life in the bread and cup. This did not arise out of any doctrine of the incarnation. Rather the doctrine of the incarnation was read out of experience in the eucharist.

Eucharist and Common Meal

The New Testament contains a large number of references to the eucharistic celebration, but only one description of "the breaking of bread" after the account of the ascension, at Troas, and this is tantalizingly slight (Acts 20:7–11). It is perhaps unfortunate that so much in St. Paul's letter to the Corinthians, which we have cited

An agape or love-feast represented in St. Callistus, Rome.

extensively earlier, is directly or indirectly connected with a dispute about the manner of "eating the Lord's Supper", but the context of the dispute is taken for granted. An impression is conveyed that all the Corinthian Christians were accustomed to assemble in the house of one of their members for a common meal, and that "the Lord's Supper" was part of this. It may be so, there is other evidence for early Christian communal meals, but it seems probable that in this case the meal was not taken in common. There was a common meeting, to which members brought their own refreshments. They were not generous, and while some had nothing to eat, others drank too much. They had forgotten the solemnity and significance of the occasion, and had to be reminded of it in strong terms. They had been "profaning the body and blood of the Lord. Let a man examine himself, and so eat of the bread and drink of the cup. For anyone who eats and drinks without discerning the body eats and drinks judgment upon himself" (I Cor. 12:27–9).

The trouble seems to have arisen through the presence in the Christian community at Corinth of someone with a room large enough to hold them all. He did not entertain them, but gave them space to eat their own meals. They went ahead and did not wait for one another, and this led to disputes and to a want of regard for the true purpose of the assembly, "to eat the bread and drink the cup of the Lord".

The situation at Troas has also been written up because of trouble, but this was probably much more normal. Whatever we think of the Acts of the Apostles as an historical record, the author was familiar with crowded meetings: "on the first day of the week, when we gathered together to eat bread", with "many lights in the

48

Eucharistic prayer in the catacomb of St. Callistus.

upper chamber where we were gathered", some sitting on benches, some on the floor, some on the window-sills, while St. Paul talked on and on until after midnight. His discourse was interrupted by a crash as a young man called Eutychus, who had dozed off, fell out of the window backward, and suffered concussion. The meeting continued with the breaking of bread, followed by further conversation until morning.

Here "the breaking of bread" has already become a technical term. "Breaking bread from house to house" (as in Acts 2:46) does not mean a common meal but a holy snack, a gathering to share a loaf and a cup, in obedience to Christ's command, as this had come to be understood, with prayer, praise and thanksgiving. This came to be associated with regular meetings after the manner of a Jewish synagogue. The Epistle of St. James refers to problems of seats and stools at such meetings, and to the dangers of obsequiousness in making way for rich subscribers, but makes no direct reference to a eucharistic climax. In another letter his brother Jude uses the word *agape,* which in later terminology means a communal meal, though substantially the same passage in the Second Epistle of St. Peter quite clearly refers to a church meeting where the testimonies, exhortations and prophecies of some members of the church are open to grave objection. Both refer to carousing, Jude in verse 12, and the author of II Peter, in Chapter 2, verse 13. It is clear that some drinking is going on, as is habitual in all gatherings, and that this has got out of control, but the passage found in both is not clear evidence of a common meal at the meeting, either distinct from the eucharist or combined with it. A common meal assumes room for all to sit or to recline, and in gatherings of early Christians this was not at all usual in the first century.

Low Mass in the catacombs as imagined in the nineteenth century.

Opposite: This Wieskirche was designed and built in 1745–54 around a painting of the scourging of Christ, which had become a place of pilgrimage, near Steingaden in Upper Bavaria. In the 'Rococo' design of Dominic and Johann-Baptist Zimmermann the fluid architecture itself seems to dissolve in ornament.

The Synaxis or Synagogue Service

All the books now used in the Synagogue are derived from the *Seder Rab Amram,* composed in a Jewish school at Sura in Babylonia, in response to inquiries from Spain, as late as the ninth century A.D. What we know of the worship of synagogues in the first Christian century is largely derived from the New Testament, supplemented by other scanty sources of information. The most notable difference between the early Christian synaxis or church meeting and what came to be the classical form of the Jewish Synagogue service is that the former began with lessons, testimonies and preaching and proceeded to prayers, while the latter begins with blessings and prayer. Some of the blessings and prayers in the present Jewish orders are undoubtedly of great antiquity, but it is not perhaps certain that their present position in the service was the original one. One reason for the Christian order is evidently to allow inquirers and hearers, not yet admitted to membership of the Church, or to any formal preparation for this, to listen to lessons, testimonies and preaching before they are ready to join in the prayers of the faithful. In the period of

50

the New Testament the element of "godfearers" and fellow-travellers in the congregation of many Jewish synagogues was evidently important, and there may well have been some who were not encouraged or even allowed to stay for the prayers. On the other hand in Eastern Churches there are blessings and prayers at the beginning of the synaxis, before the liturgy of the word, in all the developed liturgies, and some of these, in some places, may be very early indeed.

The lessons in the Synagogue were from the law and the prophets. The psalms were commonly sung in the synagogues as in the temple, and other lessons from other books were sometimes added, but these "hagiographa" were not yet a closed collection in the time of Christ, and it is often not at all clear whether "the psalms" means the hagiographa, including Ecclesiastes, the Song of Songs, and the prophecies ascribed to Daniel, or simply the psalter called "the Psalms of David". What is clear is that when the Jewish canon became fixed in the early years of the second century A.D., the Christian collection of hagiographa remained flexible, and so came to include, besides those Aramaic and Greek books that were eventually classed as *apocrypha,* accepted by Catholics and by the Eastern Churches, but not by the Churches of the Reformation, other books of their own. These were not at first classed as Scripture, which in all the earliest Christian Churches means the law and the prophets. Other writings, Jewish and Christian, were added for edification, beginning with the psalms, that had often been sung, and the Hebrew and Aramaic hagiographa that had often been read before in the synagogues of the Dispersion. St. Paul's Epistles emerged as a collection, without the pastoral letters to persons, and without the Epistle to the Hebrews, a long time before the four gospels appeared as a unit, superseding all others, and defeating attempts to collate them into one.

The traditional order of reading is the order of their acceptance. It is not as has sometimes been said, a reversal of the Jewish custom of proceeding from the lesser Scriptures to the most important, the law. All the epistles, including the letter to the Hebrews, were originally testimonies to be read at the church meeting, at the point where the reading of the scriptures ends, and their exposition begins. That this was a regular feature of worship in the synagogues of the Dispersion is clear from Acts, where St. Paul takes advantage of it to accept invitations. The nature and form of these is clearest in Chapter 13, verse 13: " . . . after the reading of the law and the prophets, the rulers of the synagogue sent to them, saying, 'Brethren, if you have any word of exhortation for the people, say it.' So Paul stood up", as any other visiting rabbi might have done, and preached a sermon on the Scriptures.

Acts itself may be read as a collection of such expositions of the Scriptures, exhortations and testimonies to the work of Christ by St. Peter, St. Stephen, St. Paul and others, set in a narrative framework from which they could be extracted at need. The gospels grew out of the same necessities, which explains some of their emphasis on the fulfilment of prophecy. They were meant to be read at meetings where the law and the prophets had been read before them. At first it seems that St. Matthew, St. Luke and St. John were gospels read in particular Churches, with other gospels, two or perhaps three of them among Jewish Christians, that never gained more than a local prestige and survive only in fragments. St. Mark's gospel,

Opposite: Rembrandt's impression of the meeting at Emmaus, where Christ after his resurrection 'was known to them in the breaking of bread' and 'vanished out of their sight'.

the oldest of the canonical gospels, had the least prestige. It was saved from oblivion by being collected with others, all with some claim to represent the testimony of the apostles. The Greek St. Matthew was commonly supposed to depend on an older Hebrew source connected with his preaching, St. Luke was connected with the Acts of the Apostles, in which the author represented himself as a companion of St. Paul, St. Mark with St. Peter's preaching, and St. John with the testimony of "the beloved disciple", commonly, and probably rightly, identified with the apostle St. John. Of the "apocryphal gospels", not included in the New Testament, those that continued to be read and translated into other languages were concerned with the Virgin birth, with the infancy and childhood of Christ, and with his mother's life and death. These became part of the tradition of Christendom, but other apocryphal gospels and acts of the apostles were discarded.

In the earliest Church all the Scriptures were of the Old Testament. The law and the prophets were the lessons of the Synaxis, with psalms and other hymns, Jewish and Christian, sung before and between them. Long after on such solemn occasions as the Vigils of Easter and Pentecost, a long series of prophecies continued to precede an epistle and gospel. In some Syrian churches there are still normally six lessons, three from the Old and three from the New Testament. Most likely at one time there were four prophecies, as at the Vigils. The four lessons of the Egyptian Copts are now nearly always from the New Testament, but the pattern of four is derived from a time when lessons from the law and the prophets preceded the epistle and gospel. In the West until recent years a similar process has led to the elimination of the Old Testament except on special occasions when a "prophecy" served for an epistle. The epistle and gospel took the place of the law and the prophets in the Synagogue. Now on Sundays there are three lessons, one always from the Old Testament.

After the lessons followed testimony and preaching, prophecy and prayer. In the early Church as in a modern charismatic context speaking in tongues can be interpreted as prophecy or as prayer. The problem of discernment between true and false prophecy took a new turn in the second half of the second century, when the Montanists prophesied the return of Christ at a date and place, which proved to be a mistake. By refusing communion to their followers who went up country to camp out at Pepuza in expectation of the end of the world, the bishops in the cities of western Asia made membership of the Church depend on loyalty to them and to their presbyters. Other Churches hesitated to support them for some time, and when they finally did so some went into schism, including the Latin writer, Tertullian.

By this time we can safely speak of the Catholic Church as an institution with a common form of diocesan government and regular communication between the bishops at synods or by letter, since synods could not be regular in conditions of persecution. Everywhere the bishops normally presided at the eucharist, blessing the bread and cup with their presbyters round them. Presbyters might preside in their absence, not because they were more important than deacons, but because these were otherwise employed with the distribution of communion to present and absent. Penitents under discipline, as well as hearers and catechumens, and in some

churches *energoumens*, awkward characters held to be suffering from some kind of demonic obsession or possession, were excluded not only from communion but from participation in the prayers of the faithful. These were dismissed before the end of the synaxis, and this came to be a more important break than the one between the synaxis and the eucharist. The first part of the service came to be called the *missa catechumenorum*, and the second the *missa fidelium*, where the eucharistic prayer followed the prayers of the faithful and took up their themes with something like the same freedom.

The readings belong to the *missa catechumenorum*. These normally included an epistle and a gospel, but St. Paul's Epistles and the Four Gospels were not Scripture as yet. A. C. Sundberg in his book *The Old Testament of the Early Church* (published in *Harvard Theological Studies* in 1964), and in further articles on the canon of the New Testament in *Studia Evangelica* IV (Berlin, 1968) and elsewhere, has shown that no list of New Testament books can be shown to be earlier than the fourth century, the age of the ecumenical councils and the creeds.

The synagogue found at Dura-Europos in Mesopotamia, under ruins of about A.D. 232. This illustrates unexpected possibilities for pictorial decoration in synagogues as well as in churches in the second and third centuries.

IV The Christian Mysteries

Rites of Initiation

The earliest description of Christian worship in the *First Apology* of St. Justin Martyr begins with baptism. This is addressed to the Emperor Antoninus Pius in the middle of the second century A.D., and was intended to be read by pagans. After describing baptismal instructions and preparations, and the actual baptism, Justin goes on:

Exterior of 'the baptistry of the orthodox' at Ravenna, originally built as a public bath in the fourth century or earlier.

After washing the person who has made a convinced assent in this way, we bring them to those who are called the brethren, where they are gathered together to pray for themselves, for the newly illuminated, and for others everywhere else, that we who have learnt the truth may act according to truth, and have good fellowship with one another in observance of our commandments, that so we may receive eternal salvation. After the prayers we salute one another with a kiss. Then bread and a cup of wine mingled with water are brought to the president who, taking them up, gives praise and glory to the all-Father through his Son's name and in the name of the Holy Spirit, thanking God at length for these gifts. At the end of this the whole company approve, saying Amen, which in Hebrew means "Let it be so". When the president has given thanks, and all who are present have assented, the deacons (as we call them) give to all who are there of the bread and of the wine and water over which thanksgiving has been made, and carry portions away to the absent. This food we call *eucharistia*: no one is permitted to partake but those who believe what is taught by us to be true and have been baptized for the forgiveness of sins and for regeneration, those who so live that Christ receives them. We do not take them to be ordinary food and drink, but as by the word of God, Jesus Christ our saviour was made flesh, and put on flesh and blood for our salvation, so also, as we are taught, the food that is blessed with thanksgiving by the word of prayer proceeding from him, food whereby our flesh and blood is nourished, is the flesh and blood of Jesus who was made flesh.

Descriptions of baptism and the eucharist together are also found in the *Apostolic Tradition* of Hippolytus of Rome (*c.* 217), in some early lives and legends of saints, and in lectures to candidates for baptism, especially in the *De Sacramentis* and the *De Mysteries* of St. Ambrose, delivered in Milan not long before 400. The details differ. What is common to Italy and Syria is the central place of the baptismal eucharist and so of the Easter Feast, when most Christian converts were baptized, in the order of the Christian year. The fast before this in Lent arose out of the preparation of catechumens for baptism, as baptized Christians gave them moral support, which gradually became an obligation. When adult converts grew fewer, Easter continued to be the feast of the blessing of the font, when many children baptized at home were brought for a final exorcism and anointing, followed in the baptistries of Italian cathedrals by confirmation at the hands of the bishop, who would be present to make the sign of the cross on their foreheads with chrism. In the East, where infant baptism soon developed a liturgy of its own, with its own preparation and conclusion, this signing could be done by the priest who baptized the child, and at any time. After baptism infants are immediately communicated with a spoon, and they continue to make their communions until they are liable to sin. In early times this happened in the West. The roots of a different emphasis are to be seen in a letter (his *Epistle* 64) of St. Cyprian of Carthage in North Africa in the middle of the third century, to deacons who complained of mothers who wanted their babies baptized immediately, in the first week after birth. He allowed this as a form of "clinical baptism", already given to sick and dying catechumens, but as the state of

emergency was allowed to extend to any infant who might die at any moment, the emergency became the normal method of baptism, and a strong argument for the view that original sin is displayed in crying. The original emergency was probably the anxiety of Carthaginian mothers who had themselves been dedicated as infants to Astarte and feared her vengeance on their babies if they did not obtain maximum protection for them.

In the East, on the other hand, the communion of infants was an obstacle to the development of eucharistic adoration. To Eastern Christians the real presence in the eucharist is first of all a physical reality, their earliest refreshment after their mother's breast. This may lead them to speak with sympathy of Protestant ideas of a presence in the faithful receiver, but in their tradition most of the faithful receivers are generally infants who may even resent the real presence in the gifts, but communion in their liturgies remains the climax, even when the adult communicants are simply the ministers.

The Sunday Mass

After his account of the baptismal eucharist in chapters 65–6 of his *Apology,* St. Justin continues, in Chapter 67:

Over all that we offer we bless the maker of all things through his Son Jesus Christ and through the Holy Spirit. And on the day called Sunday all who dwell

Russian pilgrims in the Jordan at Easter, 1908. They bathe where Christ was baptised, wearing the shrouds in which they will be buried.

Opposite: The decoration of the baptistry of the orthodox was probably begun by Bishop Neon about 458.

in a city or in the country round it have a meeting in one place, where the memorials of the apostles and the writings of the prophets are read, as time allows. When the reader has finished, the president by word of mouth gives instruction and encouragement in the following of the beautiful things in the readings. Then we all stand up and pray together, and then, as we said before, at the close of the prayers bread and a cup of wine with water are brought, and the president offers prayers and thanksgivings in a like way, for as long as he can, and the people respond, saying Amen. Then the giving and receiving of the things for which thanks has been made takes place. They are given to everyone present, and sent to the absent through the deacons.

An account follows of collections made "for orphans and widows and for those who through sickness or for other reasons are in reduced circumstances, for those in confinement and those who have travelled from afar". All these are assisted by the bishop from voluntary offerings.

This brief account has given rise to much controversy between the advocates of a written liturgy and those who hold that all early Christian prayer was free. It was probably written in Rome, with the church of the city in mind, as appears from the reference to travellers from a distance, who were constantly arriving in the capital in search of work or of opportunities to pass on somewhere else, to the learning and holiness of the East or to new prospects in the undeveloped Western provinces. The bishop of Rome was a very important person, and likely to take firm control of testimonies and preaching at the church meeting, which might be cited in other places as authorized by him. But even in Rome Hippolytus speaks of the church meeting as a place where we hear God speaking through "the teacher" and "the Holy Spirit abounds". In other churches, large and small, testimony and instruction were certainly given by other persons beside the bishop. But there must have been a great difference between great Churches like Rome and Antioch, and the small country Churches envisaged in the *Apostolic Church Order* or *Statutes of the Apostles,* where twelve Christian families require a bishop, two presbyters, three deacons, a reader and three widows, two to receive revelations if need be, and one for works of mercy. No doubt in some of these little Churches women were forbidden to pray or prophesy at a meeting, following St. Paul's instructions to Corinth (in I Cor. 14:34). But in others the prophesying widows put up their veils, in accordance with another passage in the same letter (11:5–10), where St. Paul said that "if a woman will not veil herself, let her cut off her hair", but also that "any woman who prays and prophesies with her head unveiled dishonours her head". These obscurities and discrepancies were not a great problem so long as St. Paul's letters were not regarded as Scripture.

Communion at home

Here the *Apostolic Tradition* of Hippolytus does much to illuminate the reference in St. Justin to what would now be called "reservation". It is carefully laid down that the faithful Christian should receive communion "before he eats anything else". Care must be taken that no unbeliever has access to the "eucharistized" elements, or "a mouse or any other animal, and that none falls and is lost. For this is the body of

Christ, to be eaten by believers, and not to be despised". The bread brought from the church meeting, perhaps already dipped in the blood of Christ, is kept in a cup, which is blessed again before communion, "for having blessed in the name of God, you received the antitype of the blood of Christ". This means that wine was poured in over the bread, and considered consecrated by contact, for if the cup were spilt the communicant would "become guilty of the blood of Christ".★

We need not suppose that this manner of reserving and receiving the eucharist was ever universal, but something like it was certainly common in North Africa and Egypt as well as in Rome, and probably elsewhere in East and West. The problems of communion in times of persecution, when a drive to hunt down Christians was going on, were made easier in one way and more difficult in another by the practice of communion at home. It was easier to maintain a eucharistic life than modern Christians might expect, because the cup could be filled with wine again and again without renewed contact with the bishop and presbytery. But this put the responsibility for giving and refusing communion on those who kept the eucharist in their homes. We must not suppose that all Christians were allowed to do so as a matter of course. Tertullian warned his wife that if (as he rather expected) she married again after his martyrdom (but he died in bed), her pagan second husband would want to know "what you taste secretly before all other food". Especially in times of persecution, reputable Christian householders could not always be trusted to refuse those whose communicant status was in doubt. Problems arising out of kinds of conformity with the requirements of the state or of a pagan family could not easily be settled while the bishop was away and the presbytery could not meet. Some were restored to communion under pressure from confessors, released without any surrender, who would not have reached this prestigious dignity if the government had not decided that martyrs were an asset to the Church, but confessors could be a liability. Released, they could cause confusion by claiming equal status with presbyters. Persecutors were beginning to discover by trial and error how the Churches worked.

This no doubt contributed to make bishops chary of giving permission for communion in the home, but towards the end of the fourth century there were still Christians in Rome who made their communion daily in their own bedroom as soon as they got up in the morning. St. Jerome in his letter to Pammachius would neither condemn nor approve, but he evidently thought it improper to communicate directly after sexual intercourse. Nevertheless, occasional references to communion at home continue, generally, though not invariably, in stories of monks, hermits and other holy men and women who carried the eucharist with them in a chrismal or *perula,* or kept it reserved in their cells. Regulations continued to be made against irreverence and against the abuse of the *eucharistia* for purposes of magic. Perhaps a deeper cause for distrust was the possibility of a eucharistic life independent of any particular church, if the holy chalice itself was the means of consecrating any more wine poured into it with a blessing, even if all that was left of the blood of Christ was a holy smell or stain. Yet the principle of consecration by contact was not denied. It appears most clearly in the ritual of the *fermentum.*

★All this is to be found in Chapter 32 of Dom Gregory Dix's edition of *The Apostolic Tradition of Hippolytus.*

Pope Innocent I, writing in about 416 to Bishop Decentius of Gubbio in Umbria, refers to the practice of sending a fragment consecrated at the pope's Mass to "the presbyters who cannot be with us because of the people entrusted to them . . . that they may not think themselves separated from our communion".* This *fermentum* is sent to the presbyters of the city churches, not to those outside the city boundaries who have authority to consecrate. In the city itself it was taken by acolytes to the presbyters who commingled it in the chalice with other bread. The implication is that communion in the city churches is, like communion at home, derived from the bishop's Mass.

Another survival of the same principle is the liturgy "of the pre-sanctified gifts" on days when the full liturgy is not used. These are numerous in the Eastern Churches, but in the Roman rite they came to be limited to Good Friday. The idea of the Mass of the pre-sanctified is that a liturgy of the Word, with lessons and prayers, is followed by the Lord's Prayer and communion from the reserved sacrament. This is put into a chalice, as it was for communion at home, and until the recent changes wine was poured in. In Eastern Churches this "commixture" is regarded as a consecration, and it was so regarded in the West by many in and after the ninth century, when the liturgist Amalarius defended the view fervently.† However, in the scholastic period consecration "by contact" became a point of contention in the schools of Paris and elsewhere. In the rubrics of the Tridentine Missal the reverence given to the wine on this occasion is distinguished from eucharistic adoration. But, as we shall see, the language suggesting consecration by contact at the commingling of the elements, *haec commixtio, et consecratio*, was not eliminated until the last revision. A door was left ajar that could be opened again to meet the needs of the faithful where communicants are many and priests few.

Diversity in the Eucharistic Prayer

Diversity in the early Church was greater than we can easily imagine. We know something of differences between Rome, Alexandria and Carthage, three great Churches in great cities which certainly influenced one another. All three also received influences from Jerusalem and Antioch, and no doubt more than we know from other great city Churches, like Ephesus, Smyrna and Caesarea in Cappadocia. These city Churches had common problems that did not arise in the intimate community of a Syrian, Egyptian or Cappadocian village. These again were different from each other, and from Christian villages in Calabria, Umbria and Ireland. All these received influences from the cities, but some of them gave as much as they got. Syrian village Churches in particular had a style of corporate life of their own which would be impossible in a city, long before the end of the persecutions. Features of their style of life and architecture spread into the cities later. Again monasticism, whose influence on the liturgical life of the Church has been immense, began in Syrian and Egyptian village Churches.

One important practical difference between country Churches and those in great cities is that in a country village everyone knows what everyone else is doing. It is practical to plan for a eucharist before it happens, and indeed to bake bread of a

*In *Patrologia Latina* 20 (Paris, 1845), cols. 556–7.
†Ibid., 105, col. 1152.

This baptistry of the sixth century at Povec in Yugoslavia has no font now in use. It is open to the air, and probably retains much of the atmosphere that has been lost through the diversity of decorations and usage in the baptistries of Ravenna and of other Italian cathedrals.

convenient size and shape for ritual breaking and distribution. This could easily be done and a cup or cups filled with water and wine before the synaxis began. The sacramental elements, so prepared, could be introduced at any convenient point after, or even before, the catechumens and penitents were dismissed. It was not necessary to wait until after the prayers of the faithful were finished. The Roman custom of preparing the altar and making up the chalice immediately before the eucharistic prayer is clearly attested in the middle of the fourth century. It may well be very much earlier, for in Rome a number of Churches in the houses of fairly well-to-do Christians with a large *atrium* or hall, where a considerable congregation could be collected, were certainly flourishing before the time of Constantine, when the Church began to take over public buildings no longer needed, and to erect other new buildings designed for Christian worship. But it is probably a mistake to regard the Roman method of preparing the chalice as a survival of an original separation between the synaxis in one place and the eucharist in another. Rather it arises out of the perpetual problems of city Churches where the congregation fluctuates from Sunday to Sunday.

This is important for the history of eucharistic consecration, because where the bread and wine are prepared beforehand and brought into the assembly after worship has already begun, they have a symbolic role before the eucharistic prayer. They have already been set apart for their holy use before they are definitely designated as the body and blood of Christ. In some cases it may be that they included a fragment reserved from a previous eucharist, or a *fermentum* from the

63

bishop's Mass that would, at some point in the rite, be mingled with bread and wine that were being eucharistized, blessed and consecrated for the first time in this particular Mass. It does not seem that this was ever a universal custom, but it is a natural way of expressing the unity of the Mass beyond space and time. Those who were accustomed to communicate at home in eucharistized gifts, mingled with more wine, poured in with a blessing, might well have thought it appropriate that something from the gifts consecrated at the last Mass, or at another Mass in the same local church, should be included in the new offering. This custom may not have been very common, but it may help to explain something of the reverence with which the prepared elements came to be received at their entrance into the church, not only in Eastern rites, but in some places in the West.

The idea of a change, of a conversion of bread and wine into the body and blood of Christ, was certainly not a new one in the time of St. Ignatius of Antioch or St. Justin Martyr; its roots are in the New Testament. But the idea of a moment of consecration was slow to develop, and did not develop everywhere in the same way. Where, as at Rome, the elements are prepared at the altar immediately before the eucharistic prayer, the prayer itself is the decisive point where they become sacred. Even then, the point in the prayer at which they become the body and blood of Christ may not be immediately clear to everybody. At Rome ceremonial attention to this "moment of consecration" dates from the thirteenth century. But where they are holy already, the role of the prayer in their consecration will be conceived differently.

Early Eucharistic Prayers

Research into the history of the canon of the Mass began in the seventeenth century. Western liturgists, Catholic and Anglican, had a common need to prove the antiquity of fixed forms of worship against the objections of those Protestants who maintained that in the primitive Church all prayer was extemporary and free. Catholic scholars did not deny that the Roman canon as a composition had a history. Anglicans were anxious to get behind it and to reform their own worship on primitive models, older than the Roman canon. Both Catholic and Anglican scholars knew that the Roman Church had worshipped in Greek. In looking for what could have been the Greek form of the Roman liturgy, they were naturally inclined to find something like the uniformity of their own day.

The most favoured material for a reconstruction of early liturgy from the seventeenth to the nineteenth century was the eighth book of a compilation called the *Apostolical Constitutions*. This contained a liturgy ascribed to St. Clement of Rome, the same St. Clement who wrote on behalf of the Roman Church to the Corinthian in around 96, and is commonly numbered third or fourth in the list of popes after St. Peter. Extravagant claims made for the whole compilation by some who considered it an authority superior to the New Testament were counter-productive, in that they drew attention to clear signs of Arian influence. It is probable that the *Constitutions* reached their present form around 380, at the end of the Arian controversy. But it remains likely that some of the liturgical and disciplinary material in them was much older. Some of this was found elsewhere in

This basilica of the sixth century at Povec in Yugoslavia has been little used and little altered since barbarian invasions cut it off soon after it was built.

other forms. After long researches, two of the sources were firmly identified, the *Didache* or *Teaching of the Apostles* in 1875, and the *Apostolic Tradition* of Hippolytus by E. Schwartz in 1910, and independently by Dom R. H. Connolly in 1916. Both contain eucharistic prayers. The date of the *Didache* is still problematic, and the prayers in it are still often assigned to the *agape*, not to the eucharist. It is interesting, however, to observe that in the readings of the new *Divine Office* for Wednesday in the fourteenth week of the year they appear under "the Eucharist" as a title. The eucharistic prayer in the *Apostolic Tradition* is certainly intended for the use of a bishop who has just been ordained. It is included in the order for his ordination. It is not, however, the liturgy of the Church, or of any Church. Freedom in the composition of prayers is not only assumed, but prescribed: "The bishop shall give thanks according to what we have given. It is not at all necessary for him to say the same words, as though reciting them from memory, when he gives thanks to God.

Let each pray according to his gift. If he has the gift of praying at length and with solemnity, this is a good thing. But if anyone prays briefly, there should be no objection. What matters is that his prayer should be orthodox."

Hippolytus was certainly at odds with Callistus, who was pope from 217 to 222. It is likely, though not quite so certain, that he was set up as an anti-pope in opposition to him. All that is known of this schism is by inference from his own writings, and from a statue of him sitting on a throne with a list of his books at the base of it, dug up somewhere in Rome in 1551. This is sufficient evidence that he was regarded as a bishop; in lists of martyrs he is sometimes a bishop, sometimes a priest. We have no evidence that other bishops supported him, or that he ever ordained one. If he ever used the prayer in the *Apostolic Tradition*, it was at the ordination of another bishop, or conceivably at his own. It is certainly proper to such an occasion. Much of his book refers to situations that can otherwise be shown to be specifically Roman, but he was probably not himself of Roman origin. While his prayer at the ordination of a presbyter is the basis of the one now in use, the eucharistic prayer in his book bears no great resemblance to later Roman liturgy. It is, however, one of the sources of the liturgy in book eight of *The Apostolic Constitutions,* of the Ethiopian *Anaphora of the Apostles,* and in the new order of Mass of the second eucharistic prayer.

This is in the context of an ordination. "When he has been made bishop, all shall offer the kiss of peace. . . . Then the deacons shall present the offering; and he with all the presbytery laying hands on it, shall give thanks, saying . . . ." Three responds follow, of which all have come to be in general use, not always in the same order:

> The Lord be with you.
> *And with your spirit.*
> Up with your hearts.
> *We have them with the Lord.*
> Let us thank the Lord.
> *It is right and fitting.*

In later prayers this is generally followed by some commemoration of the work of God in creation, leading to the *sanctus*: "Holy, holy, holy is the Lord of hosts. Heaven and earth are full of glory." St. Justin Martyr's description of the eucharistic prayer in his *Dialogue with Trypho* (c. 41), some sixty years earlier, refers to such a commemoration: "Jesus Christ our Lord ordered us to do this in remembrance of the pains that he endured on behalf of those who are being purged from all evil, in order that we should at the same time give thanks to God for having created the world with all that is in it for man's sake, and also for setting us free from the evil in which we had formerly been, by destroying utterly the principalities and powers through him who according to the will of God became subject to suffering."

There is nothing of this in the prayer of Hippolytus, and no sign of the *sanctus*. Some would say that the *sanctus* is a late arrival in Western liturgy. Other prayers apparently without it are cited in the late fourth or early fifth century by an Arian arguing with Catholics from their liturgy. It may be that Hippolytus did proceed

A near-Byzantine impression of the Last Supper in a mosaic at St. Apollinare Nuovo, Ravenna, Italy, of the sixth century.

immediately from "right and fitting" to thanksgiving for Christ, but the fragmentary prayers cited by the Arian already say: "It is meet and right to give thanks to you, here and everywhere, holy Lord, Almighty God." Something of the kind, with or without the *sanctus*, may be assumed in the prayer of Hippolytus. In the text he writes:

And then he shall continue thus:

> We give thanks to you, God, through your beloved child Jesus Christ, whom in the last times you sent to us to be our saviour and redeemer and the angel-revealer of your will. He is your inseparable Word, through whom you made all things, and in whom you were well pleased. From heaven you sent him into the virgin's womb, there to be conceived and made flesh and shown to be your Son in the manner of his birth from the Holy Spirit and the Virgin. Fulfilling your will and preparing for you a holy people, he stretched out his hands for suffering that he might redeem from suffering those who have believed in you.
>
> When he was betrayed to a voluntary passion that he might destroy death, break the bonds of the devil, tread down hell, enlighten the just, set up the goal for us to seek, and display the resurrection, he took bread. . . .

In this part of the prayer there are parallels to the thought and expression in other works by Hippolytus. It is probably his own composition. The account of the institution of the eucharist is brief: "He took bread and gave you thanks, saying

67

'Take, eat; this is my body, to be broken for you'. Likewise the cup, saying 'This is my blood, shed for you. In doing this, you make my memorial'." The next sentence seems to be proper to the occasion: "Mindful therefore of his death and resurrection we offer you bread and a cup, thanking you because you have found us worthy to stand before you and minister", as a bishop and presbyters in the Church.

To the next part parallels have not been found in the works of Hippolytus, but they abound in later liturgies: "We pray you to send your Holy Spirit on the offering of your holy Church, and gathering us into one, to grant that all who partake may be filled with Holy Spirit for the confirmation of faith in truth, that we may praise and glorify you through your child Jesus Christ, through whom glory and honour be to you with the Holy Spirit in the holy Church now and ever and for ages of ages."

The conclusion is probably already a standard ending for a eucharistic prayer as "Up with your hearts" is a standard beginning. The invocation of the Holy Spirit before this is more controversial. Those who first identified the prayer as by Hippolytus were surprised to find it so early, before the development of the doctrine of the Trinity had called attention to distinctions between the Word and the Spirit in action. Some welcomed it as anticipating what appears more clearly in the liturgy in book eight of *The Apostolic Constitutions:*

We beseech you to look favourably on these gifts set forth before you, O God who needs no offering. Accept them in honour of your Christ, and send down upon this sacrifice your Holy Spirit, the witness of the sufferings of the Lord Jesus, that he may show this bread to be body and this cup to be blood of Christ, that those who partake may be confirmed in piety, attain remission of sins, be liberated from the devil's guile, be filled with Holy Spirit, made worthy of Christ, and obtain eternal life through reconciliation with you, Almighty Lord.

In the Mausoleum of Galla Placidia, at Ravenna (fifth century). This sarcophagus is said to be the tomb of her husband, Constantius, who died before her about 421. The motive of the Lamb dominates.

Opposite: St. Miniato in Florence still has the air of an early basilica.

This is certainly based on a Greek text of the *Apostolic Tradition,* not necessarily as it came from Hippolytus himself. Neither prayer is for the conversion of the elements from bread and wine to body and blood, but rather that the Spirit may show to the communicants and fulfil in their communion what has already happened, that they may be bound together into unity through the Spirit in the body of Christ.

The prayers in the *Didache,* the *Teaching of the Apostles,* have been taken to be graces before and after an *agape* or love-feast, because they are so unlike later eucharistic prayers. But in book seven of the *Apostolic Constitutions* (*c.* 25), the first, in Chapter 9 of the *Didache,* is treated as a eucharistic prayer, and the second, in Chapter 10, as a prayer "after the communion". In the text of a manuscript of the eleventh century found in the library of the patriarchate of Jerusalem in Constantinople, this direction or rubric between the prayers runs: "After you have been filled, give thanks thus." This has naturally suggested a full meal, and therefore an *agape.* But both directions are interpolations by those who did not recognize that the two prayers are variations on the same themes, alternative versions of one eucharistic prayer. Both end with warnings against unworthy communion; the second: "If anyone be holy, let him come. If anyone be not holy, let him repent; *Maranatha.* Amen." *Maranatha,* Aramaic for "Come, O Lord", is out of place at the end of an *agape* or eucharist, but in place at the end of a eucharistic prayer. The first prayer in Chapter 9 ends: "Let no one eat or drink of your eucharist except those baptized in the name of the Lord, for about this also the Lord has said 'Do not give what is holy to dogs'."

Both before this have a prayer for the unity of the Church. The first is: "As this broken bread was scattered on the mountains and gathered together into one, so let your Church be gathered from the ends of the earth into your kingdom." And the second: "Remember, O Lord, your Church to deliver her from all evil and perfect her in love, and gather her together in her holiness from the four winds into your kingdom prepared for her, for yours is the power and the glory for ever." These prayers are very like the invocation of the Spirit in Hippolytus, that "gathering us into one . . . all who partake may be filled with Holy Spirit for the confirmation of faith in truth". It is true that the *Didache* does not name the Holy Spirit. But if in the *Apostolic Tradition* of Hippolytus we turn from ordination and the eucharist to baptism, we shall find that in the threefold confession of baptismal faith the Spirit and the Church are identified. Those who are to be baptized are asked at their third question, after confessing faith in God the Father and in Jesus Christ his Son: "Do you believe in Holy Spirit in the Holy Church and the resurrection of the flesh?"

In the *Apostolic Tradition* and the *Apostolic Constitutions* the Spirit and the Church are so involved that they could be confused. The task of theology at the end of the fourth century was to delimit a distinction between them by making it plain that the Holy Spirit is not a part of God's creation, but the Church where the Spirit is found is not divine. In some Churches in the West as well as in the East this led to an invocation of the Spirit, not only to bless the communicants, but to complete the consecration of the elements that they may be received as the body and blood of Christ. This did not become part of the canon of the Mass in Rome before our own time. The reason for this may be that the Roman canon took shape, as we shall see,

comparatively early, while the liturgies of the East were still in process of formation, and at a time when Rome was not so interested in making distinctions between the persons of the Trinity as they were at Alexandria and Caesarea. The Eastern Churches were in conflict with pagan forms of philosophical monotheism. The West was more concerned with cruder forms of polytheism, and with Arian attempts to adapt Christianity to these. She did not encounter Islam, or other forms of monism, until her liturgy and doctrine had settled into fixed forms for the time being. In the period of its growth belief in one God was the heart of the matter. The Trinity was treated as true, but it was not so interesting and exciting a discovery as it was in the Christian East and in some other parts of the Christian West, in Africa and Spain. In Alexandria the Spirit was invoked before and after the narrative of Christ's institution of the eucharist was recited in the prayer. At Rome a blessing was called for, but the Spirit was not mentioned by name.

V The Roman Mass

Rome

The Roman Empire has no parallel in the modern world. In terms of the time taken to reach the centre from outlying provinces, and to communicate directions to soldiers on the frontier, it was larger than the modern world. Rome itself was nearer the centre than any capital of China in the course of Chinese history. Moreover, all the citizens of Italian cities were Roman citizens as well, and most of the middle classes in nearly all the provinces had acquired Roman citizenship by the end of the second century. In order to imagine a possible parallel in the United States it is necessary to think of a capital city in the Middle West, with something like the resources and prestige of New York, and a much longer history of power.

The Church of Rome in the second and third centuries was a community of people in humble circumstances, some of them slaves, more of them freedmen who were still dependent on the patronage of their former owners. Hermas was a freedman with a market garden and a shop. He had certainly been sold as a slave by his parents, and some scholars have seen reason to suppose that he was the child of

St. Paul's without the walls at Rome, completed by 386, was very little changed before it was burned down in 1823. This and the next engraving represent its original condition.

72

Arcadian peasants, who knew that boys speaking good Greek would fetch a good price and be happier as slaves in Rome than scratching poor soil for a living at home. According to the Muratorian fragment, the Pope was his brother. This may be the work of a later writer who made the most of references to "our brother Hermas". But it is likely enough that several popes were freedmen, like Callistus, whose Christian master set him up in business as a money-changer. After his return from imprisonment in Sardinia, on charges that probably did not relate directly to his Christian faith, he looked after one of the cemeteries, probably as secretary of a burial club that served as a cover for other Christian charities. When he came to be pope in about 217 he blessed the marriage of a lady with one of her house-slaves. From this and the scandal which followed it would seem that the Church of Rome did contain some well-to-do women, not all of them willing to be widows or virgins, but nothing in the way of eligible gentlemen. The lady's relations were expected to view her conduct with extreme distaste, and with so much disgust if she had children that she might be tempted to get rid of one.

Few if any Christians were of Roman or Italian origin. At home they may have spoken many languages, Celtic, Syriac, Punic, Coptic, as many as are spoken today in an American seaboard city, but their common speech was Greek. It is likely enough that some groups of Christians in Rome worshipped in Latin before the end of the second century. They were probably of African origin, and spoke the kind of Latin that is found in Christian African writers of the period, coloured by biblical turns of phrase.

St. Paul's without the walls before the fire of 1823.

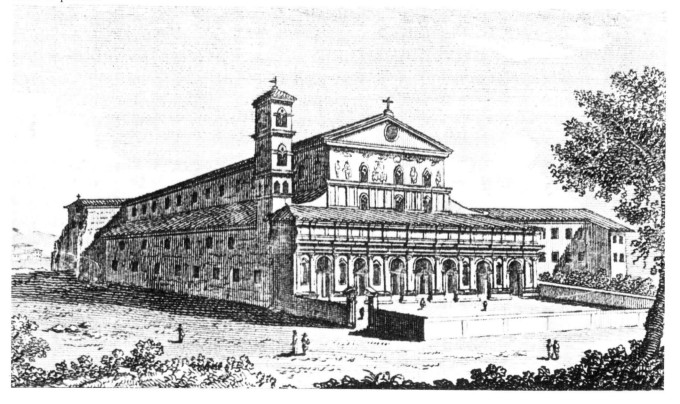

All this changed in the fourth century, but not immediately. The Roman senatorial aristocracy was still predominantly pagan in the middle of the century. The altar of Victory still stood in the Senate House, where prayers were said in the old style. Removed by the Emperor Constantius II and restored by the pagan Julian, it was not immediately removed again after Julian's death in 363. The liturgy of the Roman Church was cited in Greek by an aristocratical convert, Marius Victorinus, as late as 360, in Latin perhaps as early as 382, certainly in the closing years of the century. The Latin forms do not appear to be a translation from an existing Greek text. They have a resemblance to those found in Latin liturgies elsewhere, and probably owe something to older Latin prayers, but their style reflects the problem of making an official rite for a great public corporation in the language of government, as the Roman Church moved from the back streets to the neighbourhood of the great senatorial houses, and began to take over and use discarded public buildings. The movement is something like one from centres in the East end of London to near St. James's Park. It has been compared with the transition to the vernacular in the modern Roman rite, but although the motives overlap, the context of the concern is different. To understand it we must grasp an important difference between the diffusion of Latin and Greek.

Greek in the Roman Empire was both a literary language learnt at school and (in a rather different form) a *lingua franca* for all sorts of rough types round the ports from Marseilles to Alexandria. In this it is like English, which is both a language for schooling and examinations, and a common speech all over the world in a great variety of forms. But Latin was everywhere an official language. In the Eastern provinces it had a limited part in education, which gradually dwindled as the Empire declined, and the Byzantines lost interest in Western affairs. In the West, on the other hand, Latin superseded Greek in the schools. St. Augustine, whose Greek was not of a high standard, was acceptable as a teacher of rhetoric in Milan and Rome at a time when the Roman Mass in Latin was probably in the first stages of its formation. The Latin of the schools as taught by him and his contemporaries was an ingredient in the formation of all the Romance languages. Differences between them reflect differences in the use of Latin in various parts of the Roman Empire before this time, not only in Italy and Africa, but in Gaul and Spain and on the Danube frontier, where another kind of low Latin developed into Romanian.

In the Roman Church it is likely that while the whole congregation understood Latin in the second half of the fourth century, only a small minority spoke it correctly as it would be used in an oration in the Senate House or at a public dinner. However, these were in a class where the Church was gaining ground. Many of her ministers lacked eloquence in the official speech. They could not be trusted to improvise without disaster. Alternatives could be provided, but they must be written, and congregational response reduced to a minimum, to the Amen that is neither Greek nor Latin but Hebrew in origin, and a few other responds such as *Habeamus ad Dominum, Dignum et justum est*. The style of the Roman rite became suitable for use where a congregation knew little or no Latin. This has much to do with its later diffusion in Western Europe, although the prestige of the Roman Church as the apostolic see was also important.

Intercessions

A peculiarity of the Roman Mass as it took its classical shape is the absence of prayers of intercession outside the canon, the eucharistic prayer itself. In other liturgies intercessions may be found in three places, sometimes at the beginning, before the lessons, where the prayers are in the service of the synagogue, commonly after the lessons and preaching, where they are in the account given by St. Justin Martyr of early Christian worship, and always in the prayer for the unity of the Church in the Spirit at the end of the eucharistic prayer itself. At Rome and Alexandria, however, intercession is made for particular needs at an earlier point in the prayer; at Alexandria before the *sanctus*, in what in the West we call the preface, at Rome immediately after the preface and *sanctus*. In both Churches the dead are remembered later, toward the end of the prayer. What is peculiar to Rome and an important clue to the nature of her liturgical genius is the almost complete

The church of St. Constanza in Rome was redecorated in the fifteenth century, but retains the original structure of the fourth.

75

disappearance of any intercessions from the Mass outside the canon. Relics remain in the *Kyries* before the lessons, and in "*Oremus*, let us pray", before the offertory, where "prayers of the prone" were commonly made in the Middle Ages and "the prayer of the faithful" is now offered in the revised rite for the needs of the Church and the world.

This is the place of the solemn collects in the Mass of the pre-sanctified on Good Friday. Nothing in these is peculiar to the occasion, while much points back to the needs of the fourth century: prayer for our "most Christian emperor, that the Lord our God may make all barbarous nations subject to him for our perpetual peace"; prayer for catechumens, for heretics and schismatics; and for the conversion of Jews and pagans. "On looking at these Good Friday prayers it is evident that they are not 'prayers of the faithful'; but 'prayers for the faithful', which is quite a different thing," wrote Edmund Bishop, the great lay liturgist at the beginning of the present century.★ They are themes announced and followed by "Let us pray". The deacon then says "Let us bow the knee" and the subdeacon "*Levate*, get up". In recent times this has been done almost immediately, though the terms imply some considerable period of prostrate, silent prayer. But the people do not say anything. They are "as nearly as possible, nothing". That is characteristically Roman. These may be the original Roman intercessions at the end of the synaxis.

In the Stowe Missal, one of the earliest manuscripts of the Roman Mass – but Irish, not Roman, in origins, probably of the eighth century – prayers between the epistle and gospel are ascribed to St. Martin of Tours. These are like the solemn collects, but in the form of a litany, with responds: "We all say *Domine exaudi* and *missere domine misserre*" (*sic,* for *miserere* = have mercy). A similar litany is ascribed by Alcuin, an English scholar from York at the court of the Emperor Charles the Great, who wrote about eight hundred to the African Pope Gelasius at the end of the fifth century. Both have some of the same themes as the solemn collects on Good Friday – the Church, her priests and ministers, the emperor and his servants, virgins, widows and orphans, good weather, travellers and the sick. Two in the Stowe Missal: "*Christianum et pacificum finem* [end], we beseech the Lord to grant", and "*Et divinum in nobis permanere vinculum caritatis* [that the divine bond of love may remain in us]", and the like in Alcuin, "*Gratum vitae ordinem et probabilem exitum*" and "*Angelum pacis, et solatia sanctorum praesta, Domine, praesta*", suggest echoes of Eastern liturgies: "An angel of peace, a faithful guide and guardian of our souls and bodies", "That we may pass the rest of our lives in peace and penitence", "Christian ends to our lives, let us ask the Lord". The best clue to the place of this *Deprecatio* of St. Gelasius in the Roman Mass is a passage in the correspondence of St. Gregory the Great.† Accused of introducing Greek materials into Roman liturgy, he insisted that the Greeks use *Kyrie eleison* in a quite different way, but implicitly admits that he has introduced the *Kyries, Kyrie eleison, Christe eleison, Kyrie eleison,* where they still stand at the beginning of the Mass, as a brief substitute on ordinary days for a longer litany, probably the Gelasian one, with Greek materials and Greek responds.

Gelasius could have introduced it in this place without removing the solemn collects at the end of the synaxis, where *Oremus* continued to stand without any

★In *Liturgica Historica* (Oxford, 1918), p.122.
†*Patrologia Latina* 77, cols. 956–8.

prayers after it until today. But there are signs in the letter of Pope Innocent I to Bishop Decentius of Gubbio, already cited in connection with confirmation and the *fermentum,* that intercessions had been moved into the eucharistic prayer in Rome from a place before it. At Gubbio they were evidently accustomed to pray for those who brought up their offerings before the eucharistic prayer. A collect *post nomina,* "after the names", remains in this place in the Gallican and Mozarabic books that follow the general line of Western liturgy before the wider diffusion of the Roman Mass. It may be that prayers of this sort were offered at Rome for a time in immediate association with the offertory, after the solemn collects, or in the intervals of prayer between them. However, this was not found to be practical, but rather a source of confusion. Pope Innocent said to Decentius: "Your prudence will recognize how superfluous it is to tell God whose are the offerings made to him, since nothing is unknown to him. The oblations should be first commended, and then the names recited of those who offered them; so that they may be named among the holy mysteries themselves, and not among the things that we put before them, so that by the mysteries themselves we may open the way for prayers to come *[futuris precibus].*" The Pope did not want to hurt anyone's feelings, but it seems that the prayers in the Roman canon, for the whole Church, for the Pope, and for particular "servants of God, *famulorum, famularumque tuarum*", correspond to something that in other places, including perhaps at one time places in Rome, was done earlier at the offertory.

Something similar probably happened at Alexandria. We know that at Thmuis, in the Egyptian delta, Serapion, a friend of St. Athanasius, who was bishop there in the fifties of the fourth century, was accustomed to pray for the particular needs of his people before the eucharistic prayer, but for the dead in the prayer itself, near the end of it, when the *Memento* of the dead is in the Roman canon. In the developed Alexandrian liturgy of St. Mark there are litanies before and at the end of the synaxis, but more, including prayers for the dead, in what we call the preface, although there is some place for their remembrance at the end of the eucharistic prayer, as in Rome.

In cities like Rome and Alexandria it was important for the bishop and presbytery to exercise tight control over public prayer for particular and private needs. This could best be done if the danger spots were limited to the most solemn parts of the liturgy, where people were least likely to interrupt. In Eastern Orthodox Churches there may be much blowing of noses when patriarchs are commemorated who may be under suspicion of complacency to communism.

Varying Variations

It has been taken for granted by very great scholars that in the Latin West variation in the Mass depends upon the liturgical year. This did not take shape, apart from the Paschal feast and the season of Pentecost between Easter and Whitsunday, before the peace of the Church in and after the conversion of Constantine. It is therefore assumed that any variable forms must date from the fifth century at earliest, and most long afterwards. But many of the Masses in the Mozarabic books that until lately were still used in some places in Spain are *missae dominicales,* Sunday Masses,

St. John Lateran, the cathedral of Rome.

and in earlier missals they are not assigned to any Sunday. Neither are the Dominical Masses in the Gallican *Missale Gothicum,* or those in the earliest Gallican missal from Reichenau in the library at Karlsruhe.

In the Roman canon itself there are relics of a kind of variety that does not depend on the season in the duplication of *Te igitur, clementissime Pater* by the *Hanc igitur oblationem.* Both come between the preface and *sanctus* and the *Quam oblationem.* Compare:

Te igitur, clementissime Pater, per Jesum Christum Filium tuum Dominum nostrum, supplices rogamus et petimus, uti accepta habeas et benedicas haec dona, haec munera, haec sancta sacrificia illibata, in primis . . . . and

Haec igitur oblationem servitutis nostrae, sed et cunctae familiae tuae, quaesumus, Domine, ut placatus accipias . . .

These may be translated: "Almighty and most merciful Father, we pray and beseech you through Jesus Christ your Son, our Lord" either "to accept and bless these gifts and holy undefiled sacrifices, in the first place for . . . ." or "to be pleased to accept this oblation of your servants and all your family".

While one leads to petitions for the Church and the Pope, the other asks "that our days may be passed in peace, and that we may be delivered from eternal damnation and numbered among the saints". Both came to be recited together at the same time with a commemoration of saints in the *Communicantes* between them. But the *Hanc igitur oblationem* is found in varying forms, without the *Te igitur,* in the *Leonine Sacramentary,* a compilation of the sixth or seventh century whose provenance and authority are uncertain, although much of the material is clearly connected with Rome.

The *Quam oblationem,* which comes after them and refers back to them, has a different function from either the *Te igitur* or the *Hanc igitur oblationem.* It is cited already in the *De Sacramentis* of St. Ambrose, before the end of the fourth century, in this form: *Fac nobis hanc oblationem ascriptam ratam rationabilem acceptabilem quod figura est corporis et sanguinis domini nostri Jesu Christi.* This has become in the canon *Quam oblationem tu, Deus, in omnibus quaesumus:* "We beseech you, Lord, to condescend to make this oblation in all respects, blessed, right, reasonable, acceptable *[benedictam, ratam, rationabilem, acceptabilem],* that they may become for us the body and blood of your beloved Son, Jesus Christ *[ut nobis corpus et sanguis fiat . . .].*" *Figura* in the *De Sacramentis* is *imago et similitudo* in two very similar prayers *post-mysterium,* after the narrative of the institution, in Mozarabic masses in the *Liber Ordinum* and the *Liber Mozarabicus Sacramentorum.* These may well be based on an older Roman form, for Pope Gelasius said in a letter that "the *imago et similitudo coporis et sanguinis Christis* is celebrated in the action of the mysteries".

A like language is found in the account of the paschal eucharist on Easter night after the baptisms in Chapter 23 (in Dom Gregory Dix's edition) of the *Apostolic Tradition* of Hippolytus: "The offering shall be presented by the deacons to the bishop, and he shall give thanks over the bread for the representation *[exemplum],* in Greek the antitype, of the body of Christ; and over the cup of water and wine for the *antitypum,* in Greek *similitudo [?homoioma],* of the blood shed for all who believed in him."

Mosaic of the eleventh century,
with the death of Abel, the
discomfiture of Cain, and Noah.
(St. Angelo in Formis, near
Monte Cassino)

Similar language is found in other writers, as early and later, in two passages of
Tertullian and in the Byzantine liturgy of St. Basil, where "we have the boldness to
approach your holy altar and to set out the antitypes of the holy body and blood of
Christ." The best clue to the meaning is in one of the Gallican Masses from
Reichenau, where prayer is made: "Come down, Lord, in the fullness of your
majesty, divinity, grace, power, benedictions and glory on this bread and cup, that
these may be for us a legitimate eucharist in the transformation of the body and
blood of the Lord." Here the body and blood are transfigured into the forms of
bread and wine, "that whoever we are who take of this bread and cup, and
whenever we do it, we may receive the memorial of faith, the gift of sincere love, a
quiet hope of resurrection and eternal life in the name of the Father, and of the Son
and of the Spirit, in communion with all the saints for the remission of all our sins".
So in the classical form of the Roman canon the offering becomes for us (nobis . . .
fiat) the body and blood of Christ.

To this Calvin, unlike Luther, had no objection. As we shall see, some
theologians under his influence claimed that the Roman canon favoured their
objections to transubstantiation. In this they were wrong. St Ambrose, who in his
version of the Quam oblationem had the word figura, which they specially favoured,
clearly believed that in response to the prayer a change was made from bread and
wine to body and blood. But these theologians usefully called attention to an
imprecision in the details of the Roman canon, pointing to the time of its
composition before any eucharistic controversy.

The Role of the Narrative of the Institution

St. Ambrose and some others are cited in later controversies on the side of those who held that the words of Christ, spoken at the Last Supper and repeated by the priest in the narrative of the institution, are the form of consecration of the eucharist, and have an immediate and direct effect upon the elements; but like St. John Chrysostom, who is cited on the same side, St. Ambrose said other things in different places. The question of the moment of consecration was not urgent in the East before the Iconoclast controversy, when the adversaries of pictorial representation of Christ maintained that the eucharist was his only legitimate icon, while the defenders of icons in the other sense of pictures maintained that the eucharist was different. Before the consecration the elements might be called antitypes, figures or symbols, but afterwards they are heavenly food. This Eastern controversy had little direct effect on the West, where the problem of "the moment" became an issue in scholastic discussions of what happened if the Mass is interrupted while the consecration is going on, and of problems relating to the meaning and manner of transubstantiation. Much older than either is the idea that the narrative is an essential part of the prayer, on the same level as "Up with your hearts", "Let us give thanks to our Lord God", the *sanctus* and the Amen. This was not universally recognized in the East, but all eucharistic prayers came to contain it somewhere, even among the East Syrians in Malabar before the Portuguese got there, if some of those in the mountains of Kurdistan and Azerbaijan learnt it only from Anglicans. In the West it was recognized as a universal and necessary part of the prayer; but prayers after it continued to beseech the Lord for a blessing on what had already been decisively blessed.

Commemoration of the Work of Christ

This is nothing like so universal. In some Mozarabic prayers, what is said after the narrative of the institution is very slight indeed, while others have a good deal to say about the part of the Holy Spirit in the consecration of the eucharist. The Roman canon at this point proclaims: *Unde et memores, Domine, nos servi tui, sed et plebs tua sancta, ejusdem Christi Filii tui Domini nostri tam beatae passionis, nec non et ab inferis resurrectionis, sed et in caelos gloriosae ascensionis: offerimus.* . . . This is in line with the *De Sacramentis: Ergo memores gloriosissimae eius passionis et ab inferis resurrectionis et in caelos ascensionis offerimus* . . . in the canon "Your servants, your holy people, mindful of the blessed and most glorious passion, resurrection from hades and ascension into heaven of the same Christ, your Son our Lord, offer. . . ." At this point the *Apostolic Tradition* of Hippolytus agrees: "Mindful therefore of his death and resurrection we offer . . . .' What is offered there is bread and a cup. By the time of the *De Sacramentis* and St. Ambrose it is already *"hanc immaculatam hostiam, incruentam hostiam, hunc panem sanctam et calicem vitae aeternae"*, very much as it is in the canon, "a pure, a holy, an immaculate offering, the holy bread of eternal life and the chalice of perpetual salvation". But in the *Missale Gothicum*, where the offering is described in almost exactly the same terms, the priest continues beseeching "that you would deign to pour your Holy Spirit upon us who eat".

This invocation of the Holy Spirit is for the inspiration of those who partake, but

Abraham and the angels at Mamre, with the sacrifice of Isaac, and Jeremiah and Moses above. A mosaic of the sixth century. (St. Vitale, Ravenna, Italy)

in a Mozarabic prayer that is like it: "Remembering the most blessed passion of our Lord Jesus Christ, his resurrection from the underworld and ascension into heaven, we offer to your glorious majesty a sacrifice of bread and wine. Look on this with favour and command acceptance. Let your Holy Spirit descend on this altar to sanctify the gifts of your people, and to cleanse the hearts of those who communicate."

Post–Mysterium

It used to be said that these Mozarabic and Gallican prayers had been edited in the interests of a theory of consecration by the words of institution, and that they descend from an original or originals nearer to the Eastern liturgies, where the Spirit is invoked "that he may make the bread holy body of our very Lord and saviour Jesus Christ . . . and this cup precious blood . . .,' as in the Alexandrian *Anaphora of St. Basil,* now believed to be substantially the work of St. Basil himself, who died in 379. But such explicit prayer, that "bread may be changed into flesh, and wine turned to blood", is rare in Western liturgy. What is implied, however, in all the prayers after the words of institution in Latin books is that something has still to be done to the elements after the words of Christ. In the words of the sixth Sunday Mass in the *Missale Gothicum,* that *"Explentes sacrosancta caeremoniorum sollemnia ritu Melchesedech summi sacerdotis oblata,* we still must pray with devout mind to eternal majesty that, *operante virtute, panem mutatum in carne, puculum versum in sanguine,* we may take in the chalice what flowed on the cross from your side, Saviour." Here the bread may be changed to flesh and the wine to blood already, but the implication that the solemnities of consecration have still to be completed is still there, and it has never been eliminated either from the Gallican and Mozarabic books or from the Roman canon itself.

There the prayers *supra quae* and *supplices te rogamus* have something like the relationship to one another that has been observed in the *Te igitur* and in *Hanc igitur oblationem*. In the *De Sacramentis* they are found together: "*Et petimus et precamur ut hanc oblationem suscipias in sublimi altare tuo per manus angelorum tuorum*, as you condescended to receive the gifts of your good child Abel and the sacrifice of the patriarch Abraham and what the high priest Melchisedech offered to you."

We know from another source that Melchisedech was in the Roman canon at or just before this time. It seems unlikely that the prayer in the *De Sacramentis* is the original prayer divided later into two parts and put in a different order. As it stands in the canon in its classical form later, we pray first "that you would condescend to look at these gifts with a serene and favourable countenance and accept them as you accepted the gifts of your good child Abel and what your high priest Melchisedech offered, a holy sacrifice, a spotless oblation". Only after this do we again entreat Almighty God "to order these gifts to be brought by the hand of your angel to your altar on high in the sight of your divine majesty, that as many as receive by communion from this altar the body and blood of your Son may be filled with heavenly blessing and grace, through Christ our Lord".

The form in the *De Sacramentis* of St. Ambrose is evidently a conflation by him of these two prayers, perhaps in earlier forms, most probably made from memory. It is far more likely that he turned a single unidentified angel into the angelic host than that a single angel should emerge out of the company to carry the sacrifice to the altar on high. The single angel is almost certainly Christ himself, who is called an angel of the will of God in the prayer of Hippolytus, and constantly identified in early Christian writing with the angel of the Lord who appears to patriarchs, judges and prophets in the earlier books of the Old Testament. He himself will carry his own sacrifice to the altar on high where he ever pleads for us as our high priest. But this image of Christ as an angel might well worry St. Ambrose, who had to deal with an Arian party in his Church at Milan, who regarded Christ as a subordinate being, an archangel, not to be put on an equality with God. Both these prayers therefore are older than his version, but alternatives to one another, and perhaps to the prayer of offering just before them, at the end of the *unde et memores*, for this also ends, like the *supra quae*, with reference to the *hostiam immaculatam*, the bread of eternal life and the chalice of salvation. The Amen at the end of the *supplices te rogamus* may mark the original end of the canon.

The Saints of the Roman Canon

The prayers that follow include the *Memento* of the dead, not in all the early texts, and the second commemoration of saints, *Nobis quoque peccatoribus*. The two lists of saints in the Roman canon have attracted a great deal of ingenious commentary. It is evident that they overlap, in that the apostles and martyrs are in both, but the second seems to be supplementary to the first. The first has the Blessed Virgin, and

The sacrifices of Abel and
Melhizedek in mosaic of the sixth
century. (St. Vitale, Ravenna)

includes St. Paul among the apostles, but not Matthias, who was chosen afterward, or Barnabas, who like St. Paul was added to the original twelve. A list follows of five early popes from Linus and Cletus after St. Peter to Cornelius in the middle of the third century, and seven other saints, not all Roman, for they include St. Cyprian of Carthage and the holy healers Cosmas and Damian. The second list in the *Nobis quoque peccatoribus* adds the missing apostles Matthias and Barnabas, and among the martyrs headed by St. Stephen includes seven ladies, not all local, for Felicity and Perpetua are African, and Agatha and Lucy suffered in Sicily, but Agnes and Cecilia belong to Rome. It is hazardous to be precise about the date of either list, but it seems likely that they were put in at about the same time, and in response to pressure from those who knew of the composition of special Masses in honour of saints elsewhere. This was certainly happening in the sixth century, perhaps already in the fifth.

The Church of Rome was against multiplying variation in the canon. There must be additions to the common preface on solemn occasions. On some solemnities there may be a special version of the *hanc igitur oblationem*. There may have been days when this was said without the *Te igitur* and without any other commemoration of the living than the prayer to order our days in peace which St. Gregory the Great is said to have added to the *hanc igitur*. Very probably there were days where no *Memento* of the dead was said at the end of the prayer. The lists of saints after the names of the living had been recited, and after, perhaps sometimes in place of, the names of the dead, made it possible unobtrusively to introduce one more saint on his or her day without opening the door to an endless variety of

The Last Supper represented at Assisi under Franciscan influences; the departure of Judas Iscariot (seen top left).

special Masses on particular days. Collects before and after the readings, and after communion, were a different matter. There was no great objection to multiplying these.

The Canon and its History

That the canon had a history was known when the *Liber Pontificalis* was put together in the sixth century. The circle of Pope Symmachus, who died in 514, had much to do with its composition. If, as is possible, he had a hand in the introduction of one or both of the lists of saints, his friends may have been anxious to call attention to other popes who had made innovations in what was coming to be regarded as a fixed prayer. In the West the alternative to fixed liturgy was the kind of variation that we find in Gallican and Mozarabic missals, where every Mass has, besides collects, psalmody and readings, an *illatio, contestatio* or proper preface, prayers after the *sanctus,* and prayers *post-secreta* or *post-mysterium,* and before and after the Lord's

Prayer. The Roman rite moved in this direction with the multiplication of proper prefaces in some of the texts of the early Middle Ages, and it may be that originally it allowed more scope for variety after the *sanctus*, not only in the *Hanc igitur oblationem* on special occasions, and in the commemoration of the saints and of the names of the living and the dead, before the canon took its classical form from the *Te igitur* to the *Supplices te rogamus*. This was fixed before the time of Pope Vigilius, who in the middle of the sixth century sent to Bishop Profuturus of Braga "the text of the canonical prayer", with additions for Easter, to show "in what places something suitable for festivals may be added". The bishop kept the letter, but unfortunately lent the enclosure, which has been lost. It has been conjecturally reconstructed from places where Roman prayers *post-sanctus* are found in the *post-mysterium* of Spanish Mozarabic books. In two in particular, the *Liber Ordinum* and the *Liber Mozarabicus Sacramentorum,* the substance of the *Te igitur* is followed by prayer for those "whose oblation you deign to make blessed, right and reasonable" as in the *Quam oblationem, "que est imago et similitudo corporis et sanguinis Ihesu Christi Filii tui Domini ac redemptoris nostri",* as in the letter of Pope Gelasius and in substance in the *De Sacramentis* of St. Ambrose. These prayers are in the *post-mysterium*, after the narrative of the institution. In Spain at any rate, and very likely in Rome, there was no sense of a great difference between praying for

The communion of the apostles painted by Justus of Ghent in the ducal palace at Urbino, in the States of the Church, about 1470. Judas Iscariot is on the left, and the figures on the right are conspiring against Christ.

87

the acceptance of the oblation before and after the Lord's words, "This is my body" and "This is my blood", had been spoken.

Devotions before Communion

The correspondence of St. Gregory the Great with John of Syracuse has already been cited in connection with the *Kyrie eleison* in the history of intercessions in the Mass. It is clear in the same correspondence that he made some change in the position of the Lord's Prayer. His letter has been read as meaning that he thought the apostles consecrated the eucharist with the Our Father alone. More probably he means that they broke the bread and gave communion immediately after the prayer of consecration. If anything more is added to the eucharistic prayer of oblation while the eucharistic elements are still on the altar, it ought to be the Our Father, and nothing else.

There is evidence that everywhere, including Rome, the Lord's Prayer had long been regarded as the prayer before communion. It is so used in the Mass of the pre-sanctified; and it was probably used before communion in the home. It is the one prayer that every good Christian knows by heart. St. Gregory probably moved it from directly before the communion to directly after the doxology at the end of the eucharistic prayer. This doxology itself has traces of a prayer for the blessing of other gifts, of "all these things, O Lord, that you are always creating". This is still the place of the blessing of the holy oils in the Mass on Maundy Thursday. Perhaps St. Gregory wished to discourage the faithful from bringing miscellaneous objects for a blessing at this point by making the action more continuous between consecration and communion.

There are signs of contention about the place of the Peace in the letter of Pope Innocent I to Decentius. In the *Apostolic Tradition* of Hippolytus it is, as in St. Justin Martyr, before the eucharistic prayer, where it is in the Gallican and Mozarabic books, but in North Africa it was certainly before the communion in the time of St. Augustine, and probably earlier. This was almost certainly the Roman place when the rite was turned into Latin, but the relation of this to the fraction, the breaking of bread, is not so clear. When there were many communicants at every Sunday Mass the fraction may well have been a long and complicated ceremony. When the numbers declined on ordinary Sundays there was in some places a tendency to elaborate the ceremonial and to introduce a complicated symbolism. This would not be in accord with the genius of Rome, and it may be that the shift of the Our Father was part of a whole movement to speed things up with the sign of peace before the fraction. The older order may well have been Our Father, exchange of embraces, communion. This would be natural in communion at home, where members of the family communicated one another, and at church it would give an opportunity to the congregation to arrange themselves for communion, and for those who did not wish to communicate to slip away. By the time of St. Gregory more left before communion on an ordinary Sunday than was the case two centuries before, when the Roman Mass took shape. The reasons for this are complicated and may be better considered with the diffusion of the Roman rite to places where general communion on ordinary Sundays had never been the custom.

It is clear that at Rome the development was gradual. In the time of St. Gregory it was still customary for those who did not communicate to leave before communion took place. He may have wished them to join in the respond, *Sed libera nos a malo*, at the end of Our Father, and in the Peace that followed. The fraction and commingling, which later came after the Lord's Prayer and before the sign of peace, were probably postponed.

The Syrian Pope Sergius, who at the end of the seventh century introduced the chanting of the *Agnus Dei*, "O Lamb of God who takes away the sins of the world", in the time of the fraction, may have favoured giving this more ceremonial elaboration, as in the Mozarabic Mass and some liturgies in the East. In the Syrian *Liturgy of St. James*, which would be familiar to him, the celebrant says at the fraction: "Behold the Lamb of God who takes away the sins of the world for the life of the world." It is also possible that he was protesting against the decision of the Byzantine Council in Trullo (692–3) to forbid the representation of Christ in the form of a lamb in the interests of the growing vogue in the East of the pictorial representation of Christ *Pantokrator*, the all-ruler. If so, in the conflicts that led to the Iconoclast controversy in the next century his sympathy may have been with those who preferred symbolical to representational art. Nevertheless, Rome came down on the side of the icons. In any case the *Agnus Dei*, directed to Christ himself in the consecrated bread that is now being broken, points forward to a kind of eucharistic adoration that began in the East but went much further in the West as adoration of the consecrated host became the dramatic climax, not the communion.

The Diffusion of the Roman Mass

This, as we have seen, began early. The form of the Roman Mass made its diffusion easy. All that was needed was a sacramentary containing collects for each Mass and a limited number of variations in the preface and *post-sanctus*, and the invariable canon which could be learnt by heart. The lessons could be found in Scripture, the psalms and chants in Graduals and Antiphonaries where much variety persisted. In some places, where there were no singers, they were not used. In others songs from other rites remained. These, with more variety in the prayers, were less easily diffused. Even in their original centres they were displaced, where the canon was concerned, except in a few parts of Spain remaining under Moorish rule until the end of the Middle Ages, and in Greek monasteries in Italy and Sicily.

The Roman rite came straight from the tombs of the holy apostles and martyrs, from the apostolic see in the centre of the civilized world. In the course of its diffusion it acquired a good deal of fresh material, and to much of this the popes had no objection; but when the enlarged book came back to Rome, some though not all the excrescences were pruned down. Significantly, the number of prefaces accepted in Rome, and therefore generally, was limited in comparison with the number in some early books, including the *Leonine Sacramentary*. The canon, sometimes called Gelasian, sometimes Gregorian, remained substantially what Vigilius sent to Profuturus, and St. Gregory the Great used, at any rate where the words were concerned. The important later changes are in ceremonial, but this does more than words to fix the meaning of a ritual.

VI The Mass in the Middle Ages

The Roman Rite and British Missions

The mission of St. Augustine of Canterbury, who was sent by Pope St. Gregory the Great to Britain in 596–7, was a rare example of the Roman see taking an initiative in missionary policy. St. Augustine did not come to Rome for a blessing on his missionary vocation. He was prior of a Roman monastery, sent on the mission because the Pope trusted him – trusted him too much, since he turned back, and asked that his monks "should not be compelled to undertake so dangerous, toilsome, and uncertain a journey," and on later occasions he needed encouragement to take decisions on matters on which St. Gregory clearly intended that he should use his own judgement. In the matter of liturgy he was told to select and compound what he found suitable in the uses of Rome, of the Gallican Churches, and any others, and "so to make up a pot for the English table." In his dealings with other bishops he was warned to do nothing in Gaul except with the cooperation of the Metropolitan of Arles. However, in Britain he might expect to find unlearned

St. Guthlac takes the tonsure; one of the regular episodes in a life of a hermit saint, when he enters the clerical order. (From a manuscript in the British Museum.)

bishops to be instructed, weak bishops to be strengthened, and "perverse to be corrected by your authority."

We know little or nothing directly of St. Gregory's sources of information, but his plans for dioceses suggest that he thought of Great Britain as comparable in size to Sicily. He makes no reference to Ireland, but it seems not unreasonable to suppose that he thought of the British Isles as something like the islands of the Aegean, an archipelago in the ocean. He probably considered the Irish monks, whose proceedings were already giving rise to problems in Gaul, to be "from Britain" in this wider sense. He probably knew that they had bishops – but bishops in monasteries, dependent on their monastic superiors, with insufficient authority, and that their notions of a proper cycle for calculating the date of Easter were old and obsolete. He also knew that they could be obstinate in defence of their own customs. But he did not intend to precipitate conflict. That conflict would come was to be expected, but he would rather hear of it from his own intimates than from bishops in Gaul affronted by the extravagances of the Irish, whose zeal surpassed their own.

Bede, who tells the story of the beginnings of controversy in Britain, writes from the Roman side, but does not conceal his opinion that St. Augustine's pride in his superior civilization was partly to blame. The matters most in dispute were the date of Easter, the rites of baptism, and co-operation in the conversion of the English. The matter of the tonsure, of the proper cut for a monk's hair, seems to have arisen later. It was pressed by partisans on the Roman side, perhaps on the other, but not by St. Augustine. The baptismal question is generally regarded as even more obscure than the origin and precise cut of the Celtic tonsure, though it is illuminated by the absence from Irish liturgical texts of any reference to catechumens or penitents, or to a distinction between the Mass of the catechumens and of the faithful. We may safely suppose that, as a matter of principle, the Irish baptized first and instructed afterward those who had made up their minds that this way of life was the right one for them. They dealt with moral difficulties through counsel given in monastic communities, and the imposition of exercises of fasting and prayer by a spiritual director. They did not keep catechumens waiting for baptism, or dismiss penitents from the liturgy with them.

In practice, missionaries from Rome were obliged to do much the same. No doubt they insisted on some form of catechumenate before baptism, on a course of exorcisms leading up to anointing with the oil of exorcism, but they had not the resources to give much instruction to their many converts, whose language they hardly understood. A hundred years later it had to be said that public penance, as it was practised in Rome and Gaul, did not exist in Britain. In this and in other matters they had to learn from their adversaries. In the matter of the tonsure, while they denounced the Celtic form of haircut as an invention of Simon Magus, the archmagician and adversary of St. Peter in legends of the apostles, they developed an awareness of the importance of some recognizable sign of dedication on the heads of ecclesiastical persons that has no parallel in earlier ascetic literature elsewhere. According to Bede, St. Theodore of Tarsus, "the first archbishop whom all the English church obeyed," "had before the tonsure of St. Paul, in the manner of the orientals," but "waited four months for his hair to grow, that it might be shorn into the shape of a crown," before he was ordained by Pope Vitalian on March 26, 668, and set out on the long journey from Rome to Britain, where he died in 690 at the age of eighty-eight. It seems conceivable that this "tonsure of St. Paul," elsewhere unknown, was actually seen in Britain on the head of St. Theodore or one of his associates, and had to be suitably explained; or it may be that the African abbot Hadrian, who had been told to take care of him "that he might not, after the manner of the Greeks, introduce anything contrary to the faith into the Church where he presided," had told him first of all to be careful of his hair.

The tension between priests and bishops based on Celtic monasteries, where bishops laid hands on monks to continue the role of Druids and bards in Celtic civilization, as guardians of rite and tradition, and the regular bishops of dioceses which had taken shape while the Roman Empire was still standing, began in Gaul before St. Augustine's mission to Britain. In England it was brought to an end by St. Theodore. He did not recognize the orders conferred by "bishops of the Scots and Britons, who are not catholic on Easter or the tonsure." Bishops and priests ordained by them must be "confirmed again by the imposition of hands." But while "he often used to say that . . . only for great necessity" would he ever change the decrees of Rome, he allowed those reconciled with the Church to be immediately ordained. His tact in dealing with such saints as Chad, the apostle of Mercia, and Hilda, the Abbess of Whitby, who educated so many of the northern clergy, got him into trouble with St. Wilfred and other vehement partisans of Roman uses, and has won him an undeserved reputation among English church historians as the spiritual father of Anglican comprehensiveness. He better deserves to be called the founder of the English nation, for he made one national Church in seven or more kingdoms. He was also the creator of a model of missionary activity in northern Europe, based on direct dependence on the authority of the apostolic see.

The English missionaries on the Continent in the seventh and eighth centuries, St. Willibrord in Friesland and the great St. Boniface, organized provinces and dioceses outside the ancient frontiers of the Roman Empire on the English model, with larger dioceses than St. Theodore himself would have wished, by the direct authority of the Roman chair. St. Boniface, like St. Theodore, came into conflict with Irish monks and wandering bishops, who had penetrated to places outside any existing diocesan organisation, but also with diocesan bishops in the Frankish kingdom who were unwilling to conform with his interpretation of the rule of Rome. He made an alliance with Pepin the Short, the "Mayor of Palace" of the King of Austrasia and Neustria, and assisted him to displace the Merovingian dynasty, which had long lost effective power among the Franks, and to replace it by his own family, with the moral support of the Pope in Rome. In return King Pepin came to the assistance of the apostolic see against adversaries in Italy, and took the first steps toward the establishment of the Papal States as a Roman zone in Italy, belonging to "the republic of the Romans," the clergy and notables of Rome, but not to the Roman Empire, whose government in Constantinople was at odds with the Pope over the Iconoclast controversy.

Opposite: The ivory cover of a sacramentary made for Bishop Drogo of Metz about 850, with scenes from the Mass to be read from top to bottom of each column. On the left, the entry, gospel and offertory; on the right, the signs of peace and communion; in the centre, the consecration.

Carolingian Liturgy

The alliance between the Franks and the Roman see persisted under Pepin's son, the famous Charles the Great, Karl or Charlemagne, who reigned from 772 to 814. In 800 he came to Rome to rescue Pope Leo III from adversaries and was crowned by him as "Emperor of the Romans". A group of scholars around his court at Aachen included an Englishman, Alcuin of York, who did much to frame the future pattern of liturgical and canonical regulation in the Latin West of Christendom.

The Franks intended to be loyal to Rome, and imported Roman books to serve as liturgical models. A sacramentary sent to Aachen by Pope Hadrian I in 791, and expanded with a supplement derived from Gallican and earlier Roman sources, became the basis of Roman liturgy as this was understood in the High Middle Ages, not only in the north but in Rome itself. This *Gregorian Sacramentary* was a papal book, originally intended for masses celebrated by the Pope himself or by bishops who stood in for him. This was by no means the first sacramentary to have a considerable circulation north of the Alps. The *Gelasian Sacramentary*, originally intended for the use of presbyters in the "titular" churches, the city churches in Rome, survives in a number of adaptations made at a distance from the city, in Italy, Gaul and Germany, before and after the time of Alcuin, and certainly long after St. Gelasius or St. Gregory the Great.

In the course of the ninth century a number of manuscripts of the *Ordo Romanus*, containing accounts of ceremonies in Rome, with particular attention to such solemn occasions as the Easter Vigil, or Mass at an ordination, were in circulation beyond the Alps. But those who went to Rome to discover what really happened, like Amalarius, whom we have already encountered inquiring into the consecration of wine in the chalice by contact with the precious blood, often found that the *Ordo* which they had read was in conflict with Roman practice. It does not therefore follow that the books represent a more ancient use. When this kind of book is copied, it is always transcribed for a practical purpose. The transcriber, especially if he is a liturgist, will often include in his text much that he does not understand, in the hope of discovering more later, and much that does not belong to the original but to the *Use*, in a technical sense, of the monastery or cathedral for whose use the *Ordo* is being copied.

Through fifty years, from about 780 to the thirties of the ninth century, under Charlemagne and his son, Louis the Pious, the court of the King of the Franks was the chief centre from which Roman liturgy was diffused in an Anglo-Frankish version, coloured by Gallican and Irish influences, over western Europe. The Carolingian pattern survived, and was renewed at the court of Charles the Bald among the Neustrian Franks in the third quarter of the ninth century, and at the same time and a little later in the Wessex of King Alfred, who among the kings of the time was singular in having the instincts of a scholar. He wrote and translated books himself. It was renewed again under his grandson, King Athelstan, and under Edgar the Peaceful, the friend of St. Dunstan. It came back again to west Germany and Lorraine with Otto I, who was crowned emperor in Rome in 963, with his grandson Otto III, and with Henry II and Henry III in the eleventh century. But Europe through all this time was torn by internecine strife between the descendants of Charlemagne and their nobles, and plagued by invaders, the Magyars of Hungary before they were converted to Christianity, and above all the Vikings, the Scandinavian pirates from Norway, Sweden and Denmark. Effective government was reduced to more and more limited localities. The popes were increasingly preoccupied with the defence of their own estates against Moorish raiders or Italian noble adventurers, when they were not reduced to the situation of ceremonial priest-kings who performed the rites for a secular ruler. Ambitious Italians saw in control of the papacy the key to power in central and southern Italy.

No one could make the papacy into an instrument of dynastic policy without coming into conflict not only with ascetic enthusiasts in Italy and pilgrims from beyond the Alps, but with everyone who needed to appeal to Rome against the abuses and oppressions that were the natural consequence of the general anarchy. Those who needed Rome most included the kings of Germany, accustomed to work closely with the bishops and abbots, who were their most reliable public servants in conflicts with the German nobility. When it came to the division of dioceses, or to the need to make new arrangements about the disposition of ecclesiastical property and rights, a single bishop or an abbot and convent could be very difficult. In such conflicts the apostolic see was the ace of trumps and could not be left permanently in the hands of the local Roman nobility. So from time to time the King of Germany crossed the Alps for his coronation with the iron crown as King of Lombardy, and with the imperial crown at Rome. He brought Frankish influences, and generally he secured some advantage to take back with him, but he could not stay for long.

Monastic Liturgy

Meanwhile the future of liturgy lay in a few monasteries where enclosure could be maintained and the life of prayer developed in spite of disorder in the world. Such places grew rich, if their reputation as places of prayer was good, not only because lords gave them or left them lands, but still more because refugees from burnt-out farms came to squat in clearings within reach of them. Much of Europe was then unoccupied, even within the old imperial bounds where the population had probably declined steeply since the fall of the Roman Empire. Much of the forest in southern Germany, of which some still remains, had never been cleared. Where monks went in search of peace, others followed in search of comparative security. Vikings indeed and Magyars did not spare monasteries, but they were not directly involved in private wars and faction fights, in which combatants might well hesitate to violate their territory and so bring curses on themselves and prayers for their enemies. The consequent wealth was itself a peril to the religious life, for it attracted aspirants seeking comfort and safety. Hard labour was no longer needed when baskets of corn and vegetables were constantly brought in by grateful tenants, themselves probably refugees, glad to have found a place to live under a saint's patronage. The new danger was that monks would be bored. They had to be employed.

Cluny in the Duchy of Burgundy was not the only abbey that became a centre for liturgical development in the tenth and eleventh centuries. There were others in

Cluny as seen in the last days of its glory, by J. B. Lallemande in 1773. Most of its buildings were destroyed in and after the French Revolution.

Lorraine, and also in England, associated there with St. Dunstan, who moved from the Abbey of Glastonbury to become Archbishop of Canterbury, and St. Oswald, who established cathedral priories at Worcester and York. What is singular about Cluny is its independence from royal or episcopal patronage in a time and country where royal power was at a low ebb. In an age when the papacy was almost entirely absorbed in local concerns, the Abbot of Cluny became head of a confederation of dependent priories, the model on which all the later religious orders were founded. The Benedictines were at this time a number of independent monasteries following a common rule. The Cluniacs were Benedictines who followed the rule in a form mitigated by the authorities of the Carolingian age, in contrast with the later

An early representation of Low Mass in an oratory, from a manuscript of the ninth century.

Cistercians, who claimed to be returning to primitive Benedictinism. But both Cluniacs and Cistercians were orders as the "black" Benedictines were not at this time. They came to have congregations later, when they needed to organize, in the age of the Friars, the Franciscans and Dominicans, who came after the Cistercians and the Premonstratensian canons, from whom they had learnt much.

In descriptions of the customs of Cluny for Cluniac priories★ we see distinctly a new division between the major Mass, which is influenced by the papal liturgy, as this was understood by the Frankish liturgists in the ninth century, and celebrated at different times of the day according to the season, an additional Mass that was also celebrated in common on feasts in Lent and on some of special distinction that might fall in the ember days of fasting, and other Masses sung by individual priests with one or at most two *socii*, or servers. At Masses celebrated in choir by the whole convent there would be a subdeacon and deacon to read the lessons, and provision could be made for the chants proper to every occasion. But at private Masses the priest sang everything, including the lessons and chants, and servers only responded. These could be sung without special permission before and after Prime and until Terce, which from Easter until September was generally followed by the major conventual Mass. To sing them after this Mass permission was generally needed, although in winter they could be sung without special leave until after the bell rang for one or other of the Masses sung by the convent later in the day. Provision had to be made for a clash in obligation between a private Mass and the daily offices of prayer. The idea evidently was that Masses could be sung in intervals between the offices, between Prime and Terce at 9 o'clock, between Terce, the major Mass, and Sext at noon, or occasionally after that. Because in the absence of clocks or watches the hours of offices were only approximately accurate, those who had begun to prepare for a Mass were allowed to go on and complete it if they had already put on a stole when the bell for an office or for conventual Mass rang. In that case they were

★By Bernard in *Vetus disciplina monastica*, ed. Marquart Herrgott (Paris, 1726), and by Ulric in *Patrologia Latina* 149.

excused, and need never ask pardon for missing the other obligation. But if they had not yet put on a stole they must stop and go into choir.

Architecture reflects these developments in the growth of a circle of small chapels around the ambulatory at the east end of abbey churches and cathedrals, and soon at other places, in aisles and transepts. Much later they spread into parish churches. Liturgy reflects it in two ways, in the elaboration of chants for "high" Masses, especially of sequences and "proses" between the lessons, and in the incorporation in the Mass of what were originally private devotions. This is difficult to document, for it must have happened before there are any signs of it in the manuscripts, and much was probably not written down before the invention of printing. However, the preparation of priest and server by mutual confession and absolution before Mass arose in this period, as did the multiplication of prayers at the offertory. At Cluny priests were forbidden to move their lips while putting the host on the paten, lest saliva should slip out. There it seems that the chalice and paten were prepared at the offertory, as in Rome, with provision at high Masses of five hosts, "that those who wish may be able make their communion." But in other places the chalice was often prepared beforehand, at the beginning of Mass, as at Westminster Abbey, or between the epistle and gospel, as in the rite afterward followed by the Dominicans. This could lead to further elaboration in prayers for the acceptance of the offering, when the chalice and paten are prepared and again when the sacred elements are taken for consecration, preliminary to the prayers in the canon itself. The passion for mystical meanings led to the further elaboration of distinctions between these.

In the earlier of the two surviving customaries from Cluny it is not assumed that all private masses are for the dead, but special prayers for the dead are enjoined if the Mass is for the living. In the later customary, which may date from the twelfth century, a conventual Mass for the dead is celebrated every day. There is other evidence that the Feast of All Saints on November 1st, and the Commemoration of All Souls on the day after, were celebrated at Cluny in the time of Abbot Odilo (994–1048), and spread from Cluny round the Latin Church.

Distinction between the commemoration of saints and of those whose salvation is in doubt goes back to a passage in Chapter 110 of the *Enchiridion* of St. Augustine: "When sacrifices are offered for the baptized dead, whether at the altar or through other kinds of alms, on behalf of the very good they are thanksgivings, for the not so very bad propitiations; on behalf of the very bad, even if they are of no help to the dead, they are some kind of consolation to the living". In the next sentence St. Augustine concedes that to sinners they are of some use, "to this extent, that there may be full remission, or that surely damnation itself may be made more tolerable." This last sentence made difficulties for medieval commentators, and it is not easy to see what the saint means. What is clear is that his whole argument assumes that there was no obvious outward distinction between Mass in a saint's honour and Mass for the soul of your grandmother.

Like conclusions can be drawn from such Masses for the dead as are found in the sacramentaries. In the *Leonine Sacramentary* they are associated with the commemorations of deceased popes; in the *Gelasian,* where all the extant copies were made at a distance from Rome, they came after Masses for classes of saints, apostles,

martyrs, virgins, confessors, in what is now called the common of saints. They
begin with two for infants and adults who have died in their baptismal innocence,
and include Masses for use in the cemeteries and basilicas when all who were there
buried were commemorated together. Mass was generally celebrated for monks on
the day of their death, which was often, though not always, the day of their funeral.
Lay people in good standing had the same service after three days, but for a penitent
reconciled on his deathbed his friends must fast for a time before Mass could be
celebrated for him. In some of the later copies of the *Gelasianum* the collects and
lessons used on this occasion were appointed for use at funerals, where prayer in a
penitential tone was considered appropriate to the occasion, for instance when a
penitent had not had any opportunity for reconciliation or when no penitential
discipline had been applied but friends feared for the soul's salvation. This same

A soul weighed in the balance.
The patron saint intervenes with
a gold chalice, representing the
Mass.

Mass came to be celebrated on the third, seventh and thirtieth days after death, and subsequently on anniversaries or "year's minds". Such uses were certainly established in many places by the time of the Carolingian Renaissance. Amalarius notes the omission of Alleluia and "Glory be to the Father" at Masses for the dead, as in the offices in commemoration of the passion of Christ at the end of Holy Week. But nothing of the sort happened in the East, and it is only in the eleventh century that this became the normal way of praying for any dead person in the West. Even then the funeral rites of the Mozarabic *Liber Ordinum* keep the note of Easter joy that remains dominant in the East, but was absent from rites from the dead in most of the Latin West, except in the very rare instances where the deceased was already regarded as a saint, from the twelfth century until after the Second Vatican Council.

The origin of this characteristic note of dread is not easy to explain. Edmund Bishop in a "liturgical note" added to an edition of *The Book of Cerne,* made by Dom A. E. Kuypers and published in Cambridge in 1903, connected it with the Irish, probably rightly, but some of his arguments are criticised by Dom Antoine Chavasse in his edition of *The Gelasian Sacramentary* (1958). What is clear is that the diffusion of ideas connected with All Souls comes from Cluny.

In this connection a story is told in different forms by writers of the eleventh century, of a regular visitor to Cluny from somewhere in Brittany, or somewhere else on the coast of Aquitaine, who on one of the Greek islands, or in another version somewhere in the Sahara, encountered an anchorite like St. Antony of Egypt, who had intimate knowledge of the demonic world. He told him of the wrath of the demons "whom I have often heard lamenting . . . because by the prayers of monks and by alms for the poor . . . again and again by the mercy of God the souls of the condemned are freed from their pains." He wished the monks of Cluny to know that especially great complaints were made against them and their Abbot Odilo, "whereby they may more and more persist in prayers, vigils and alms for the repose of souls in pain, that thereby joy may be multiplied in heaven and grief and loss inflicted on the devil".

Raoul Glaber, who was probably the first reporter of this, makes him go on to say: "Such power has the constant offering of the life-giving sacrifice that hardly a day passes in which this business does not rescue souls from the power of malignant demons." Glaber himself goes on to comment: "It is indeed the custom of that monastery, as we have ourselves observed, from the first dawn of the day until lunchtime, on account of the number of brethren, to celebrate Mass continuously." In the customaries this is put rather differently, but the total effect is much the same, that Masses may be said before Prime, and in the intervals between the conventual Mass and the offices, until a time of the day determined by the season, which more or less coincides with the first refreshment taken in the refectory.

I do not think that Glaber made up the story, but he edited it to connect it with a pilgrimage to Jerusalem, and to put the anchorite in a suitable place on the way back. Jotsald, the biographer of Abbot Odilo, who probably used Raoul's account, moved him from a Greek island, where he might be a schismatic, and set him somewhere in Africa, making the traveller a persistent explorer of distant places.

This was painted in Flanders in the fifteenth century, and represents a miraculous manifestation of the flesh of Christ during a celebration of Mass by St. Gregory the Great at the Sessorian basilica in Rome. The story is told by his two biographers of the ninth century, Paul and John the deacon.

But both agree that he came from somewhere on the west coast of France. It is impossible not to suspect that the anchorite was of the Irish type, and lived on one of the islands off the coasts of Brittany or Cornwall, or even in Connemara.

The reason for this is that both imply that his revelations were responsible for the introduction of All Saints and All Souls into Cluny. There must be some connection between this and the Celtic feast of Samhain at the end of the agricultural year, when cattle were slaughtered for the winter, and the dead were believed to appear and to share the feast. Another story connecting Christian and pagan rites for the dead relates to a companion of King Arthur, who was caught and mortally wounded by a dark figure when he stole a candelabrum from a perilous chapel. King Arthur went to the same place and saw a Mass served by the Virgin herself, who offered her Son to be crucified on the altar, and then received him back as he was before. One version of this story is in a history of Glastonbury by John, a monk of the abbey,★ and relates to the cemetery there, an ancient holy place where grave goods were discovered and might be variously interpreted. It is a form, perhaps the oldest, of the story of the Holy Grail.

Controversial Devotions

This and other stories of a bleeding Child seen in the Mass are associated with a type of piety that came under criticism in the ninth century, and again in the eleventh, from theologians who had studied the writings of St. Augustine. Their criticisms were rediscovered at the time of the Reformation and identified by Catholics and Lutherans alike with aspects of the teaching of Zwingli and Calvin. There is no reason to believe that the Swiss Reformers learnt anything from them, but in England they were welcomed by those who sought to find in early mediaeval tradition support for their criticisms of the developed doctrine of transubstantiation. This, however, was not at issue at the time. In 1059 the Archdeacon Berengar of Tours was reluctantly obliged to confess at a synod in Rome that "the bread and wine that are placed on the altar, after the consecration, are not only a sacrament but also the true body and blood of our Lord Jesus Christ, and sensibly [*sensualiter*], not only in sacrament but in truth, are held in the hands of priests, broken and bitten by the teeth of the faithful". He intensely resented this, and continued to speak against it, but twenty years later Pope Gregory VII was contented that he should say:

> I believe in my heart and confess with my mouth that the bread and wine which are placed on the altar by the mystery of the holy prayer and the words of our redeemer are substantially converted into the true and proper and life-giving body and blood of Jesus Christ our Lord, and after the consecration are the true body of Christ that was born of the Virgin and offered for the life of the world, that hung on the cross and sits on the right hand of the Father, and the true blood of Christ that was shed from his side, not only by the sign and virtue of the sacrament, but in property of nature and verity of substance.

Unfortunately Berengar's earlier forced confession of 1059 was reproduced as Chapter 42 in the second distinction in the third part of the *Decretum* of Gratian, a handbook of canon law with an appendix on theology which came to have immense authority. But it was treated very critically by Lothario da Segni in the fourth of his six books, *De Sacro Altaris Mysterio*, written before he became Pope Innocent III. He noted in Chapter 10 that the body of Christ "is not divided into parts, or torn with the teeth, since it is immortal and impassible", and cited St. Augustine in support of this. This might not be very important, as like views are expressed by theologians of as much and more personal weight, if he had not been Pope at the time of the Fourth Lateran Council in 1215, where use was made almost in passing of the verb *transubstantiare* in saying that the universal Church "the same Jesus Christ is both priest and sacrifice, whose body and blood are truly contained under the appearances [*sub speciebus*] of bread and wine, *transubstantiatis pane in*

★*Chronica sive Historia*, ed. Thomas Hearne (Oxford, 1726), pp. 70–4.

Cistercians in choir, with figures of death behind them. Two of them are mitred and crowned. From a manuscript in the British Museum.

corpus, et vino in sanguinem potestate divina; that to perfect the mystery of unity we ourselves should receive from his [nature] what he himself took from ours". The origin of the word as a theological term is open to doubt. It is found in a sermon attributed to Hildebert of Lavardin, who died in 1134, but the sermon is not his. It belongs to a rather later writer. The attribution is interesting, however, since he was a friend of Berengar, and wrote his epitaph. It is found in common use in the 1140s. In the absence of anything that could be called an official definition of its meaning

103

before the Council of Trent, it was easy to interpret it in the light of the first confession of Berengar in 1059, preserved in the *Decretum* of Gratian. Some colour was given to this idea in the nineteenth century by the discovery of an exposition of the canon of the Mass ascribed by Cardinal Mai to Peter Damiani, one of the group of Italian reformers closely associated with the papacy in 1059; but this exposition has been shown to depend on the *De Sacro Altaris Mysterio* of Innocent III. The original context of the word is therefore to be seen in a concern to insist that the presence is in *substantia*, not in *species*, in power and virtue, not in anything "sensible" or material, in fact in the very concern that Berengar shared with St. Augustine and with an earlier Augustinian, Ratramnus Maurus, confused by him with John the Scot, a great Irish student of Greek philosophy and theology at the court of Charles the Bald in the second half of the ninth century.

One of the passages found in the work on the canon of the Mass ascribed to Peter Damiani, which is also found in the *De Sacro Altaris Mysterio* of Innocent III, is concerned with the order of the prayers:

> It seems that in respect to the order of the eucharistic consecration the section beginning *qui pridie quam pateretur* [on the night before he suffered] ought to have been placed at the end of the canon, since in it the consecration is consummated, but since this would have impeded the order of the historical narrative . . . the arranger of the canon, that he might preserve the order of the history, compelled as it were by a certain necessity, placed this section in the very heart of the canon . . . in the middle, so that what follows is understood as going before.

This may be one of the passages that impelled Peter of Blois, a French savant who held English benefices, to write two fervent letters to the author after he had become Pope Innocent III, imploring him to take in hand the necessary work of reform in the canon of the Mass. He complained, as Protestants did afterward, that the first part of the canon appeared to refer to a number of successive sacrifices. He explained these by the contributions made by members of the Church to the common meal implied in St. Paul's letter to the Corinthians. To pray for those "in the sleep of peace" is out of place, if the pains of purgatory are worse than anything that can happen to us in our present life. There can be no authority for interpolating the words *mysterium fidei* into our Lord's speech in the narrative of the institution. The author of the canon had relied on his own invention rather than on Scripture, and the efforts of successive popes had not sufficed to correct his errors. But the heart of Peter's complaint is that the words of the canon do not move priests to devotion or contrition. "The whole of the inner man should dissolve in tears through the recording of the agony and the crucifying of Christ, of the whole burnt offering of our redemption, of the burning of fat, as it is commanded in Leviticus." Out of the stores of his considerable learning Peter recalls the use of blood as applied to the eyes of elephants to stir them up for battle. So the record of the passion of Christ should stir up in us first of all "a contrite and humbled heart", secondly "grace to desire a holy devotion, and thirdly the will to be united in love's bonds". He turns to sacrificial scenes in the Old Testament, to "the external altar of bronze

Communion of a knight in Rheims Cathedral.

where animals, that is the beastly motions and extravagant actions of men of today are spiritually immolated", and finds there prophetic signs of confession, contrition and absolution. But he finds nothing in the canon that moves us to wonder at the wounds of Christ, at the bitterness of his passion, the piercing of his hands and feet, nothing that can really invite us to do this in his remembrance. These letters★ were written after 1202, probably in the next year, in the time of the conversion of St. Francis, before he was moved to tears in front of the crucifix in the chapel of St. Damian at Assisi. Devotion to the passion, to the humanity of the crucified Christ, was in the air already.

Innocent III did not reform the canon, but to his time belongs the first clear attestation of a change that probably began a little before and continued rapidly directly after his reign, the most important change in the Roman Mass between St. Gregory the Great and the Second Vatican Council. That is, the introduction of the elevation of the host immediately after the moment of consecration. In his time, probably about 1215, the author of the *glossa ordinaria* on the *Decretum* of Gratian, expounding the same distinction that contains Berengar's forced confession, wrote of the *Supplices te rogamus*: "It seems that this prayer is superfluous, because it is said after the words by virtue of which the body of Christ is made [*conficitur*], and hence the prayer about what has been done is superfluous. I reply: not only does Scripture not attend to such strict time limits, but the priest too, as he cannot say many things at once, so speaks as if time stood still, and as if those things had to be done which at the beginning of his speech had yet to be done." But by the end of the century any interpretation of the *supplices* in the sense of transubstantiation, that to be brought to the altar on high means to be changed, had to be rejected, "since the elements are

★See article, "Some New Letters of Peter of Blois", by R. W. Southern in *The English Historical Review* liii (1938), pp. 412–24, especially pp. 421–4.

Ci commence le oroison
E te salue tres saint et
tres precieux corps de mo
createur ihucrist et qui es

Communion of a lady in the later
Middle Ages, from a manuscript
in the British Museum.

already transubstantiated". *Haec* – these things – in the *supplices* has to mean the Church militant, to be carried through to the Church triumphant, or the supplications of the faithful, their vows and prayers, in the *Rationale divinorum officiorum* of Durantius of Mende.

There was nothing new about the idea of the words of institution as the moment of consecration, and in serious theological writers other parts of the prayer were

An altarpiece of the seven
sacraments by Roger van der
Weyden, made for Tournai and
now at Antwerp. On the left are
baptism, confirmation and
penance, on the right ordination,
marriage and holy unction in the
hour of death. The Mass is in the
centre, behind the cross of Christ.

seriously considered, but there is no doubt that the elevations did much to confirm
in popular piety the belief that the purpose of the Mass is to bring the sacrificed
Christ to us on the altar, and that the immaculate victim, the *hostiam immaculatam,* in
the *Unde et memores* after consecration, is the divine Son, the Lamb that was slain, in
a different sense from the *oblationem ratam et rationabilem* before the consecration.
Duns Scotus regarded this as the climax of the eucharistic sacrifice, though St.
Thomas in an older tradition preferred to speak of sacrifice and consecration as one
and the same. This was also the tradition of the Byzantine East, when Nicholas
Cabasilas wrote his *Commentary on the Divine Liturgy* in the middle of the fourteenth
century. He referred to "certain recent Latin writers" who no longer recognized
anything corresponding to the invocation of the Holy Spirit in Eastern liturgies in
the *supplices te rogamus* of the Roman canon. But he made a more important point in
saying that change in the sacramental elements "bears on two things, on the
condition of not being sacrificed, and on the bread as bread. The unsacrificed object,
bread, has become the sacrificed object, and simple bread has become the body of
Christ", the sacrificed body of the Lamb of God, one and the same sacrifice as was
made on the cross.

Controversy on this was quite unnecessary, as both sides recognized without
great difficulty in the Council of Ferrara and Florence in 1438–9. But the new
ceremonial emphasis on the words of institution in Western liturgy had unfortunate
side effects. It did much to reinforce the idea that the first Mass was the Last Supper,
and that any attempt to reform the Mass in accordance with Scripture must start

107

from there. Meanwhile it led to distinctions between prayer in the canon before and after the consecration of the bread and wine to be body and blood of Christ.

The Parish Mass

Chantries founded to sing masses for souls became a common form of religious endowment in the fourteenth and fifteenth centuries, superseding the friars, whose popularity waxed in the first century after their foundation, and then rapidly waned. The friars were important, where liturgy was concerned, as disseminators of the Divine Office as used in the Roman court and of the Missal of the Roman Church, not only to cathedrals and abbeys, but to parish priests in a form that they could use. Hostility between the friars and the parish clergy has been exaggerated. It was chiefly found in a few towns where the friars had churches of their own, and drew away congregations from the parishes, and in the administrative services of every diocese. There the bishop's officials found the friars difficult customers, who took from them their best potential recruits, popularising the idea that an archdeacon had little chance of salvation. The kind of man who had always intended to spend his life as a parish priest did not become an archdeacon or one of the friars, but he often heard their sermons and bought and used their books. His parish Mass had always fallen short of cathedral standards, but the friars helped him to see what could be done with a small choir of boys who wanted to be clerks. His people did not understand it, and did not listen to much of it, but they liked to know that it was going on, and generally disapproved of those who discharged their obligation to attend Mass by putting their heads into a side chapel where a chantry priest was mumbling a requiem, or waited to go to confession until a friar came and went. That lay devotion was not dead is shown by the scale of expenditure on parish churches and their furniture on the eve of the Reformation. That much of it was motivated by anxiety about the destiny of souls after death is shown by the immense endowment of chantries.

Erasmus observed on the numbers of special Masses, "the Mass of the crown of thorns, of the three nails, the Mass of the foreskin of Christ, Masses for those who travel by land and sea, for barren women, for persons sick of quartan and tertian fevers". He wrote: " . . . We must reprove the insolence of those who walk about the church when Mass is being celebrated, talking of their own private affairs, and when it is finished go and find a priest of their own to say a special Mass for them". To those who were demanding that all should participate in holy communion at Mass he said that the absence of this practice was not altogether the priests' fault.

> How can there be general communion when in many cases the churches are almost empty at the time for receiving it? Some people leave . . . even before the introit. Others leave immediately the gospel has been read, which . . . they do not understand. At the time of the Preface, after the priest has said *Sursum corda* and *Gratias agamus* [let us give thanks], then especially there should be participation with the priest in silent communion with God. Gossip in the market-place and carousing in taverns, bad as it is, is not so disgraceful as the irreverence of those who stay in church chatting during the entire service.

These comments are cited from his *De Sarcienda Ecclesiae Concordia,* written and published after the controversies of the Reformation had begun. Similar strictures, though in a lighter tone, can be found in his writings before the controversy and in those of others who were more consistently loyal to Rome than he was. A movement of reformation would have happened in any case. There was much in common between the concerns that led to the German and Swiss Reformations, and directly and indirectly, to the Reformations in Scandinavia and Great Britain, and those that led to the Counter-Reformation in Italy and Spain. The schisms between them were not necessarily inevitable, but a certain divergence of concerns between nations of Europe was already evident in the Conciliar Movement a hundred years before. These appear again in the conflicts of the Reformation.

Dürer's engraving of Erasmus (1526).

VII The Crisis of the Reformation

The Attack on the Mass

The Mass and infant baptism are both effectual testimonies to the primacy of the divine initiative in the Christian life. We are helpless when we are first baptized, and in the Mass God gives himself to us. Unhappily both can be, and often have been, treated as the operations of ministers on behalf of others. The minister of baptism, whether he or she is a priest or deacon in church or a midwife or nurse in the home, counts the number of babies saved by baptism. The Mass can be a rite performed by a priest for a prescribed intention, stipulated in the terms of an endowment.

At the end of the Middle Ages the growing number of foundations for requiem Masses provided small incomes for a large number of chantry priests, who in turn often provided a supply of cheap labour for other purposes. One of the reasons for the popularity of such foundations in market towns is that they were often associated with schools, and also provided clerks who had to stay on the spot but had no other ecclesiastical business. These for small sums would write letters and make up accounts at the end of the year. More and more things had to be done that involved reading and writing, and this was both a stimulus to the growth of elementary schools and a reason for having extra priests about who could at least write. The motives for the foundation of chantries were therefore different from those that promoted the foundation and support of good monasteries in the tenth and eleventh centuries. Then what everyone wanted was the prayers of holy men. The priests in charge of chantries as a class had not that reputation. What people wanted before they decided to found a chantry was some assurance or guarantee that the rites performed by them on their small altars, behind screens in cathedrals and parish churches, had some effect before the throne of God for the welfare of sinful souls.

The explanations provided were various at various levels. Some no doubt were what might be given today by any Catholic explaining why it would not be right for a priest to accept a number of stipendiary offerings from different people for the same Mass. But it was inevitable that, as soon as popular controversy started on the subject, the most extravagant claims for the efficacy of particular kinds of "votive Masses" would be cited by radical reformers, accused by conservative churchmen of mounting an attack on the Mass.

Luther's own criticism began with a measure of moderation. In one of his earliest popular writings, *A First Inquiry Concerning the Pagan Servitude* [*De captivitate Babylonica*] *of the Church,* he addresses "priests who offer the sacrifice of the Mass in these corrupt and perilous times", entreating them to take care "that the words of the greater and lesser canons of the Mass, together with the collects, which all too plainly re-echo the sense of sacrifice, do not refer to the sacrament but either just to the bread and wine which the words consecrate, or to their own prayers. Indeed, the

bread and wine were formerly offered to receive a blessing, and so become sanctified by the word and by prayer. After the blessing and consecration, they are no longer offerings, but gifts received from God''. ''The lesser canon'' here means the prayers at the offertory, which were all late introductions from earlier Gallican missals, said at this time in varying forms in Germany. Those that eventually came to prevail and stood in the Tridentine Missal, were cast in what seemed to be stronger language than those of the canon itself.

Luther hoped that priests in sympathy with him would bear in mind that ''the gospel is superior to all canons and collects . . . and offers no warrant for calling the Mass a sacrifice''. At a public Mass the priest's intention should be to communicate himself and let others communicate. At the same time he should certainly pray for himself and others, but ''he must take care lest he presume to offer the Mass . . . If a priest is saying a private Mass, he must conceive his action as one of communicating himself''. No one should dare to accept payment for votive Masses, or ''to presume to offer any votive sacrifice''. But if he confines himself to prayer for the living or the dead ''in this way the money will be, not for the Mass, but for the prayers, and to buy himself food and clothing''.

Luther's fundamental presupposition in all this is: ''Prayer is something quite different from the Mass. Prayer can be extended to comprehend as many people as I choose; the Mass covers none other than him who exercises his own faith, and him only in so far as he exercises it.'' The point is clearer in one of his later writings

An impression by Cranach of Protestant baptism and communion as founded in the sacrifice of Christ, as preached by Luther from the pulpit. Meanwhile, pilgrimages and austerities are recommended by the influence of a demonic anti-Christ.

Luther preaching, with an Evangelical celebration of holy communion on his right, and the powers of this world going down into hell on his left; an impression by his friend, Cranach.

where he says that even if the priest "indeed believes that in the private Mass the body and blood of Christ are produced, the layman cannot know it and must doubt and be troubled about whether he is adoring mere bread and wine". "Godless and false Christians and all devils have this belief", that it is the body and blood of Christ in the sacrament, and "it is nothing but a human idea and delusion; for no papist has the true Christian faith; they cannot have it, because they do not believe that they have grace and life through Christ alone".

This to Luther was the heart of the gospel, that the Mass cannot be given to God or to other men. "Rather, God bestows it on men through the agency of the priest; and men receive it through faith alone, apart from all works or merits. There will be few persons so foolish as to suppose that a poor man does a good work when he comes in his poverty to receive a gift from the hands of a just man, but the Mass is the gift of the divine promise." Challenged to defend this radicalism, Luther fell back on Scripture, already insisting in his *Treatise on the New Testament* (1520) that the nearer our Masses are to "the first Mass of Christ, the better they undoubtedly are; and the further from Christ's Mass, the more dangerous". This was the ground of his difference from Andreas Carlstadt and from Zwingli in Zurich, who also started from the Last Supper but drew a different conclusion from the account.

Zwingli emerged as a radical reformer after Luther, in 1521, but he had probably been thinking about the liturgical issues involved as long or longer. He was a very different character, a pupil and admirer of Erasmus, priest of the parish church in a Swiss city where the town council was in any case prone to conflict with the Bishop of Constance, while Luther was an Augustinian friar and a theological professor in a university under the patronage of the Elector of Saxony. Zwingli was already intimate with the lady who soon became his wife, first in secret, then in public, while Luther married Katarina von Bora only when it became clear that she had no intention whatever of marrying anyone else. In both cases the marriages seem to have been happier than might be expected in view of the circumstances and the stormy character of the two leaders. But Zwingli's marriage is an indication that he was already closely identified with the members of his congregation, with the hopes, desires and ambitions of ordinary lay people in the town, before the Reformation began.

Zwingli approached the problem of the Mass and the canon in a much cooler manner than Luther, analysing confusion and corruption of language where Luther denounced an abomination. He was able to show from the words of the canon that the prayer could not be primitive. Much of it must be later than the *De Sacramentis* of St. Ambrose. The Latin seemed to him more degenerate by far than that of Gregory the Great, and therefore later. It did not occur to him that St. Gregory wrote Latin quite exceptionally well. On the other hand while neither Luther nor Zwingli seem to betray any sign of acquaintance with other liturgies, with the possible exception, in Luther's case, of the Mozarabic Missal lately printed by Cardinal Ximenez, Zwingli's first attempt to draft an order of holy communion shows him surprisingly close in some respects to primitive tradition.

Luther's idea was to cut out the canon. In his Latin *Formula missae,* produced in 1523, there is no offertory and the narrative of the institution is linked with the common preface at *per Christum Dominum nostrum, qui pridie....* The words of institution are to be chanted in the tone used for the Lord's Prayer. The elements are elevated while the *sanctus* and *benedictus* are sung. Then all join in the Lord's Prayer. There is no fraction, but the peace is given, and communion with the traditional words, while the *Agnus Dei* is sung. There is to be no Mass without communicants, who must give notice beforehand and provide a satisfactory account of their faith and understanding of the sacrament, and awareness of their need of help. They are to sit by themselves apart from the rest of the congregation, so that their communion will really be an act of witness, and like priests they communicate themselves from the chalice. In his later German Mass of 1525 the *Sursum corda* has disappeared, and an expanded paraphrase of the Our Father is to be read either in the pulpit or at the altar, leading through an exhortation to the words of institution, which are still more isolated than before. The bread and cup may be blessed and administered separately, but the elevation remains, and the *sanctus* and *bendictus qui venit* as hymns to be sung at the communion.

By contrast Zwingli, who from the first made his communicants sit down as they would for a common meal, provided in place of the canon, after the *sanctus* had been sung, a series of prayers beginning *Te igitur clementissime terque sancte Pater.* The first contained a long thanksgiving for the creation and redemption of man, not unlike an early eucharistic prayer, and leading to the Our Father. The second is a prayer to feed our hungry souls with heavenly food. The third that the image obliterated in Adam may in this way receive the face of Christ, and that "as many of us as shall be partakers of the body and blood of this Son of yours may breathe in and speak out as one [*unum solumque spirent et exprimant*], and in him, who is one with you, may

Contemporary engraving of Zwingli.

A detailed impression, in a Protestant caricature, of the sale of Indulgences and other acts of the apostolic see by the authority of the papacy (portrayed as Anti-Christ, sitting where he ought not to be).

Cranach's portraits of Luther and Katharine von Bora, his wife who was to be 'saved through childbearing'.

themselves be made one''. Further prayer of the same sort leads to the narrative of the institution as a climax, and to "comfortable words"–"Come then all that labour and are heavily laden, and I will give you rest". Communion is given with an expansion of the traditional words of administration: "The body and blood of our Lord Jesus Christ preserve you for eternal life." This is clearly the source of the rites of communion in the English *Prayer Book* of 1549.

Some doubt whether this service really expresses Zwingli's intention, and is not rather, like the first English *Prayer Book,* a step on the way to further reform. It is not unlikely that without the conflict with Luther Zwingli would not have been so negative about the presence of Christ in the eucharist. He had been a follower of Erasmus, who in the work already cited in the last chapter spoke of the idea of a symbolic presence in the Mass as one that might be entertained and seriously considered at the coming General Council. From Erasmus Zwingli and other Reformers who had been under his influence, not only in Switzerland, but in Germany, Holland and England, had learnt to take seriously the idea of a plurality of sacrifices, that "every prayerful action that consists of praise and thanksgiving is a sacrifice". They quoted Peter Lombard, the Master of the Sentences, summarizing the teaching of the Christian Fathers for the schools in the twelfth century: "What is offered and consecrated by the priest is called a sacrifice and oblation, because it is a true memorial and representation of the true sacrifice and holy oblation made on the altar of the cross." This is in the fourth book of his *Sentences* (*distinctio* xii, 7).

Protestant Liturgy

It may be that Zwingli was cautious in taking steps toward a new pattern of worship in hope of a general reform of the Church. But from the very beginning he was more hostile than Luther to the traditional pieties of popular religion. His hostility

A Calvinist communion service
in Germany as represented in
Picart's collection of engravings
of ceremonies, made by a critic
with a Catholic background and
a sceptical attitude to all
traditional religion.

to the Anabaptists, who wished to treat all Papists as pagans, reveals a real leaning in
his own mind in that direction; but it was essential for the progress of the
Reformation to keep the sympathy of the citizens of Zurich and their town council,
who would be outraged if they were not assumed to be Christians. As the Swiss
Reformation developed in antagonism between Protestant and Catholic cantons,
Catholic sympathizers in Zurich, if they had a chance, took refuge elsewhere, while
Protestant sympathizers in the Catholic cantons took refuge in Protestant ones. In
the German states the matter is much more complicated on account of the different
grades of vassalage which enabled lords who held fiefs as vassals of the bishops, of
the Duke of Bavaria, and of the Emperor as Archduke of Austria or King of
Bohemia, to act as if they were tenants-in-chief of the Empire, with as much
authority to introduce the Reformation as the Electors of Brandenburg or Saxony.
The Treaty of Augsburg in 1555 had recognized the secularizations of ecclesiastical
lands made by Protestant princes of the Empire in and before 1552, and the right of
Lutherans, but not of Calvinists, to set up the Confession of Augsburg, made in
1530, as the standard of faith in their territories. After this, Lutherans and Calvinists
alike assumed that in their own landchurches they had to deal only with their own
confession, that townsfolk and peasants alike could be expected to conform. Indeed
in cities like Geneva a large part of the population came from elsewhere, while those
who could not accept the new religion and discipline had to submit or emigrate.

In consequence of this most Protestant liturgies express the theology of a
particular party with different degrees of ability. Bucer at Strassburg in Alsace, and
Calvin there and afterwards at Geneva, were counted among those who worked for
a wider Protestant alliance. Calvin in particular only came into the picture after the
division between Protestant and Catholic was an accomplished fact. No doubt he

was a mature man of considerable reading when he adhered to a Protestant confession, but he had never served the Catholic Church as a priest in any situation. In this his position stands in complete contrast with that of Archbishop Cranmer and other English Reformers with whom so many of his followers came to be associated. The closest parallel to the English Reformation is in Sweden; but developments there were so closely affected by what happened in Lutheran Germany that their importance in the sixteenth century is secondary. The role of the Scandinavians as workers for the reunion of Christendom was late in beginning, and their subsequent importance may well be due to the fact that in Norway as well as Sweden there was very little organized opposition to the Reformation, and little encouragement to resist coming from Rome. The country priests and peasants were placated by leaving the churches much as they were, with woodwork and pictures, and a liturgy in the vernacular that began much as it did before and was still called a high Mass, although more and more often it tailed off after the sermon without communion. Where communion was given it was on the lines of one or the other of Luther's rites, but with vestments and more attention to ceremonial decencies. The Scandinavian Churches still have bishops, though they are married and their wives are addressed as bishopesses.

The English Reformation is indubitably different, not because the Reformers had an entirely different intention, as Anglo-Catholic and High Church Anglicans like to believe, but because the principal authors of the movement were high ecclesiastics promoted by King Henry VIII, as prepared to promote the withdrawal of English obedience from the court and Church of Rome, after the crisis of the Reformation had already begun. Bishops like Gardiner and Bonner, whose theological sympathies were conservative, were also prepared to promote the royal supremacy "over all persons and in all causes". The opposition included men of outstanding piety and intelligence – St. John Fisher and St. Thomas More – as well as the Carthusians and a handful of monks and friars, but the great majority of

influential people, including the higher clergy, acquiesced in changes that did not at first affect the liturgy, except in a minimal way by the omission of the pope's name and of the feast of St. Thomas of Canterbury.

The *Book of Common Prayer* grew up out of the reflections of Archbishop Thomas Cranmer and some of his friends in the years between the breach with Rome and the death of King Henry VIII in 1547. They were working with others who did not share their theological ideas, but were in different degrees committed to the breach with Rome. At least one of the bishops who were commonly considered conservative, Cuthbert Tunstall of Durham, was a friend of Erasmus, and doubted the usefulness of transubstantiation as a theological term. The *Paraphrases* of Erasmus were circulated with the English Bible in parish churches in the reign of Henry VIII. In the clash between Erasmus and Luther, who denounced him as deviating from the theology of St. Augustine in his book *The Freedom of the Will* (1524) as well as in the differences between Luther and the Swiss over the meaning of "This is my Body", the "oral manducation" by the communicants of the true body and blood of Christ, and what precisely may be said to be received by the wicked, the English Reformers had divided sympathies.

It is no part of the purpose of this book to explain the attitude of such conservative ecclesiastics as Gardiner and Bonner, and of Henry VIII himself, to the breach with Rome. This is an obscure question. However, it may be useful to point out that in the vital years between 1527, when the troops of the Emperor Charles V sacked Rome, and 1547, many who were well informed were probably afraid that the Emperor would promote a reform of the whole Church on lines that suited the interests of the house of Austria in Germany, Italy and Spain. Fears in France led the French king to support at the same time resistance in Rome to any programme of reform and independent action by German Protestant princes in their own territories. Henry VIII was not in a position to influence the papal court after his schism, and his attempts to cooperate with the German princes and their Lutheran theologians did not prosper, but he was determined that whatever happened the English crown should emerge in a stronger position through the dissolution of the monasteries and the unification of ecclesiastical and royal jurisdiction in England, Wales and Ireland. He was in a stronger position than the Emperor or the King of France, in that in England not only most of the landed classes, but the bishops and diocesan clergy, were accustomed to act in cooperation with the crown. He did not want to disturb this alliance by precipitating further religious changes that might not be popular. He did not immediately observe that the circulation of Protestant ideas, encouraged by the schism and by the known sympathy of the Archbishop of Canterbury and others in high places, could not easily be stopped. After a delaying action in 1539–43 he began to take more account of this. An English Litany was introduced in 1544, and the Prince of Wales was already receiving a Protestant education when he came to the throne as Edward VI in 1547, under a council of regency from which conservative champions had been excluded by Henry VIII's last will and testament.

'Communion in a Protestant Church' by a Polish painter born at Danzig who lived in Berlin from 1745 to 1801. This represents a Lutheran celebration of the period.

The Books of Common Prayer

The Reformation under Edward VI proceeded in three stages, the Order of Communion in 1548, the *First Prayer Book* of 1549, and the *Second* in 1552. In later Anglican controversies the two prayer books are opposed, but they came from the same circle of liturgical reformers. The problem is to determine which of the changes made in 1552 were intended in 1548–9, and which were the result of controversies in 1549–51. The number of influences involved in these was large, as several sorts of Protestants converged on England in search of opportunities and offices. A few were Lutherans. Melancthon, Luther's old and prudent associate, was invited, and promised to come, but never did so. Lutherans in general, perhaps especially in his circle, feared that any compromise with the other kind of Protestant in France, south Germany and Switzerland would not only alienate the most fervent disciples of Luther, whose death in 1546 gave his fixed ideas more power, but throw away what chance they still had of coming to an understanding with the Emperor on the reform of the Church as a whole. So most of those who came to England held some variety of intermediate position between Luther, who upheld the real presence in the Mass in a literal sense, and Zwingli who was now considered to have denied it altogether. The importance of Calvin as the central theologian of Protestantism, holding the only one of these intermediate positions that was going to evolve into an internationally influential theological system, was only just beginning to be recognized. *The Institutes of the Christian Religion* had been written but not widely read.

The importance of the *Prayer Book* for the history of the Mass must be defined

An impression of the interior of a church by a Dutch painter of the second half of the sixteenth century. This illustrates the transitional period when altars were discarded, but not defaced, and pictures were still in use even where Protestantism had prevailed.

before it is examined. Of Protestant liturgies it has been by far the most influential, beyond the bounds of Anglicanism, among Puritans who took up positions against it and Methodists who used it. The real problem in considering differences between the two *Prayer Books* put out in the reign of King Edward VI, in 1549 and 1552, is not the place of the *Gloria in excelsis* or the communion devotions, but the treatment of the canon. In 1549 every part of the canon is represented in the prayer of consecration, including intercession for the Church, for the living and the dead in the communion of saints, but this has its own introduction and ending, and may well have been intended to stand where it did in 1552 and in later editions of the *Prayer Book,* after the lessons, the creed and the sermon, and before the communion devotions. The prayers at the end of the eucharistic prayer in 1549 could also have been inserted at the last moment under conservative pressure, for the same themes are found in the same order in the *Antididagma* of the canons of Cologne, prepared for them by Gropper, a friend of Erasmus, as a counterblast to the *Consultation of Hermann,* advice to Hermann von Wied, Archbishop of Cologne, by Melancthon and Bucer, a close friend of Cranmer, when he was intending to introduce the Reformation into his diocese. The *Consultation* was used by Cranmer, and the *Antididagma* may well have been in the hands of his critics.

When allowance has been made for this it remains true that the eucharistic prayer in 1549 has a *post-sanctus* and a *post-mysterium* before and after the narrative of the institution. The *post-sanctus* has an invocation of the Spirit and the Word: "Heare us (o merciful father) we besech thee; and with thy holy spirite and worde, vouchsafe to bl + esse and sanc + tifye these thy gyftes, and creatures of bread and wyne, that they maie be unto us the bodye and bloude of thy most derely beloued sonne Jesus Christe. Who in the same nyght . . ." In the *post-mysterium*: "Wherfore, O Lorde and heauenly father, accordung to the Instytucyon of thy derely beloued sonne, our sauiour Jesu Christ, we thy humble seruauntes do celebrate, and make here before thy diuine Maiestie, with these thy holy giftes, the memoryall whyche thy sonne hath wylled us to make, hauyng in remebraunce his blessed passion, mightie resurrection, and gloryous ascension. . . ." The reversal of the traditional and natural order, remembering we do, to we do remembering, could be explained by an original intention to proceed from the ascension into the doxology, "who lives and reigns with thee and the Holy Spirit". In 1552 what was left of this *post-mysterium* was put into the *post-sanctus,* where later Anglican liturgies have: "Hear us, o merciful Father, we most humbly beseech thee, and grant that we receiving these thy Creatures of Bread and Wine, according to thy Son our Saviour Jesus Christ's holy Institution, in remembrance of his death and passion, may be partakers of his most blessed body and blood, who in the same night. . . ." The prayer ends at the traditional moment of consecration, followed immediately by the communion of priest and people.

If this had been Cranmer's original intention in 1549, it is hard to see why he introduced an invocation of Word and Spirit to be removed at the next revision. It is more likely that he intended something like a Mozarabic or a Gallican Mass. He had certainly studied the Mozarabic Missal. At one point in the order of baptism the *Prayer Book* of 1549 agrees with the Vetus Gallicanum against the Mozarabic on a point of detail, and this makes it likely that some Gallican materials in manuscript were known to the English Reformers, although no texts had yet been published. The difference between 1549 and 1552, at the most important point, the disappearance of a *post-mysterium*, was almost certainly due to Bishop Stephen Gardiner, who in what Cranmer called "a crafty and sophistical cavillation" found the sacrifice of the Mass in the traditional sense in "the memoryall whyche thy sonne hath wylled us to make", in the *Prayer Book* of 1549.

In 1552 the Reformers wanted to make it perfectly clear that this was not intended. The eucharistic vestments were not to be used, and the Holy Communion was to be celebrated at a table, not at an altar, in the midst of the church or in the choir. But in Queen Elizabeth's reign the *Prayer Book* was modified again. The vestments were restored until further order, which was not taken in terms that could compel obedience. The chancels were to "remain as they have been in times past". A certain ambivalence was allowed, and even encouraged, in Anglican attitudes to what had been done in the same cathedrals and parish churches, generally by the same people, before the Reformation entered its properly Protestant phase.

This found expression some fifty years later in the second edition of a treatise *On the Church*★ by the Dean of Gloucester, Richard Field, who was able to prove to his own satisfaction that the sacrificial language of the Roman canon refers either to the

Frontispiece to Charles Wheatly's *Rationale of the Book of Common Prayer*, first published in 1710. Christ is celebrating the sacrifice on his altar in heaven like the priest below, at the north end, according to the Anglican rubric in the *Prayer Book*.

★1606, in the new edition (London 1849) vol. ii, pp. 59–65.

Frontispiece to Pierre le Brun's *Explications* of the ceremonies of the Mass (1716). Compare Wheatly's representation of a heavenly altar over an Anglican eucharist at the same time (1710) and Van Eyck's Adoration of the Lamb, *supra*, pp. 11, 121.

offering of bread and wine, of prayers and praises, or to the presentation and pleading of the one sacrifice of Christ upon the cross, and not to any propitiation distinct from this. He had noticed what Edmund Bishop, speaking of the Roman canon, called "the almost embarrassing simplicity, or even it would seem want of technical exactness of suggestion, found in details of that document; a matter which did not escape those acute, eminently able, and most interesting writers, the great Anglican Divines of the seventeenth century". This is in a long note on "the moment of consecration", attached to Dom R. H. Connolly's edition of the *Liturgical Homilies of Narsai*.

Field and others detected an element of innovation in the writings of such contemporary Catholics as St. Robert Bellarmine, who allowed that bread and wine might belong to the matter of the sacrifice, but insisted that only the body and blood of Christ are properly sacrificed through the change which they suffer in consecration and communion. They were interpreting the teaching of the Council of Trent, but not the tradition of the Church or the sense of the canon. This line of argument made an impression, according to Bishop, on Louis Billot, afterward a cardinal, who began to introduce a different interpretation of the Council of Trent. But as a defence of the continuity of Anglican liturgy it does not account for the way in which the eucharist in the Church of England became an occasional office in Field's time.

On Sunday morning the liturgy began with Morning Prayer and a litany modelled on the Litany of the Saints. Holy Communion followed, but on most Sundays it was broken off after the prayer "for the whole estate of Christ's Church militant here on earth". On the few Sundays and feasts when the celebration continued, and communion was given, those members of the congregation who were not prepared to communicate left at this point. They had already been in church longer than their fathers and mothers before the Reformation. They had never made their communions often, and many of them had scruples about the new rite. Those who wanted a proper Mass waited for an opportunity to hear one, and perhaps to make their confession and communion, when a recusant priest was next in the neighbourhood. Others who despised papistry, held that the long liturgical service was nothing but a popish Mass in English. Some of the clergy agreed with them, and worked for radical reforms. Others did not think it right or prudent to celebrate Holy Communion without a sufficient congregation, and did not hope to find one more than six or eight times in the year. Communion in the parish church was a symbol of conformity and solidarity, where some who had been described as "church papists" proved that they were not recusants, and Puritans showed that their nonconformity did not extend to separatism or schism. But it was not central to the life of prayer as the Mass had been before the Reformation. Where this has become the centre of Anglican worship in the nineteenth and twentieth centuries, this has been the result of Catholic influence. In the Anglican tradition it is peripheral and occasional.

VIII The Tridentine Missal

The Catholic Reformation

In Protestant history, which has dominated understanding of this period nearly everywhere since the French Revolution, the Counter-Reformation arises from the defeat of the Reformation in Italy by those conservative forces that in all situations oppose reforms, with the aid of powerful and disciplined reinforcements from Spain. These consolidated their position at the Council of Trent, and were able to take the offensive with fire and sword in France and the Netherlands, Germany and Bohemia, and by propaganda and conspiracy elsewhere – in Ireland and England, Hungary, Poland and Lithuania.

This interpretation confuses the northern Renaissance with the Reformation. The difference between the Renaissance in Italy and in most of northern Europe goes back into the fourteenth century, when Italians began to identify themselves with the classical past in the age of Boccaccio and Petrarch, and some Englishmen, with other northern Europeans, began to identify Italy and the papal court, first at Avignon, and then at Avignon and Rome in the period of the Great Schism in the papacy, in and after 1378, with the paganism of the classical past. This view of the papal curia became increasingly plausible in the last quarter of the fifteenth century, but the tension between northern Europe and Italy is already evident in the

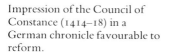
Impression of the Council of Constance (1414–18) in a German chronicle favourable to reform.

Conciliar Movement, at the Council of Constance held in 1414–18 to heal the schism between rival popes, and at the Council of Basle called for the reformation of the Church in 1431. This Council divided in 1437 between those who were anxious to meet the Greeks from Constantinople at Ferrara and afterwards at Florence, and those who wanted to maintain contact with the Bohemian Utraquists, who had defeated crusading armies sent against them.

By this time the renewal of interest in Christian antiquity was already developing in northern and southern Europe, but especially in the north, where two directions might be taken. One arose from the intensive study of those works of St. Augustine that were not generally available in libraries before the invention of printing, another from the discovery that he was not the only important Christian Father, that Tertullian, St. Cyprian and others besides those generally known in the Middle Ages, St. Hilary, St. Jerome and St. Ambrose before St. Gregory the Great, had written in Latin, and that Greek Fathers had been translated, and more Greek material should be made available in translation. This difference was already apparent in the division of the Council of Basle in 1437. Those who went with the Pope to Ferrara and Florence genuinely welcomed an opportunity to meet the Greeks. The Bohemians had themselves demanded that the Greeks should be involved in any decisions with regard to communion in the cup. Those who stayed at Basle were above all anxious to maintain the principle laid down by the Council of Constance, that a general council is superior to the Pope. In one sense the Greeks agreed with this, as did all the Orthodox East, then and now. But they could not recognize the ecumenical character of purely Western assemblies, and insisted that their meeting with the Latins should be called the Eighth Ecumenical Council. Pope Eugenius IV was prepared to agree with this, seeking to escape from the toils laid for him by some of the more recalcitrant members of the Council of Basle. Although the Council of Ferrara–Florence failed to avert the fall of Constantinople, and was soon repudiated by the Russians as well as by Greek and other Orthodox Christians under the Turks, the name remained in the records. The Fifth Lateran Council in 1512–17, which is generally regarded as the most ineffective and unimportant council in the history of the Church, was called the Ninth Ecumenical Council by Gaspar Contarini, who played an important part in the Council of Trent, in a memorial for Pope Paul III in 1533. This Lateran Council did pay some attention to Eastern affairs, consolidating the union of the Syrian Maronites with Rome. By this time all the East, except the Greek islands still controlled by Genoa and Venice, including Cyprus, was either under the rule of Muslim powers or of a very remote Czar of Russia in Moscow.

Interest in the East nevertheless continued, and was even stimulated by fear of a Turkish invasion of Italy and Germany. The contribution of Erasmus to the inquiry into Greek Christianity in antiquity was outstanding, and his influence persisted on both sides of the schism between Protestants and Catholics, long after Luther wrote against him in *The Bondage of the Will* in 1525. In Italy and Spain his friends came under suspicion because they read Protestant works with sympathetic attention. Some of them fled from the Roman Inquisition after Spanish methods of investigation were adopted in Rome. But those who took refuge with Protestants

The Council of Trent, a contemporary impression of the first sessions of 1546.

did not easily conform to their strictly Augustinian standards of orthodoxy. Some passed through Protestantism to Unitarianism. Others, however, who succeeded in holding their ground, survived to make an important contribution to theological discussion at the Council of Trent.

In Spain their troubles began earlier, in a different situation. The Spanish Inquisition had been primarily an instrument to keep in check any activity that might weaken the war effort in the long struggle with the Moors through the whole of the Middle Ages, from the Muslim conquests in the eighth century to the final conquest of Granada by the Christians in 1492. This had contributed to maintain in Spain attitudes that had become out of date elsewhere in Europe and could not easily be revived even to meet the urgent perils arising from the expansion of Turkey. Spanish scholars were accustomed to the Inquisition, rather as Russian scholars are used to the activities of the professional ideologists of the Communist Party and of the secret police. They could conceal their debt to Erasmus so thoroughly that the extent of his influence in Spain has only begun to be discovered in the present century. His concern for the freedom of the will found its most powerful channel of expression through the Society of Jesus, founded by a Spaniard who had studied him and studied to conceal his debt to him. Erasmian influences at the Council of Trent ought not to be confused with the resistance of the Italian Renaissance to any reform of discipline.

The Council of Trent

The idea of a council to reform the Church "in head and members" was in the air on the eve of the Reformation. To the idea of a Ninth or Tenth Ecumenical Council, after Florence and the Fifth Lateran, the idea of a council free, Christian and German came to be opposed. "Free" in this context means uncontrolled by the papal curia; "Christian", to judge in accordance with apostolic tradition, however this is conceived; "German", in awareness of the centres of crisis in Wittenberg and Zurich. The choice of Trent was a compromise; a German town on the Italian side of the Brenner Pass, acceptable to the Emperor, who would not accept Mantua or Vicenza, and tolerable to the Pope as accessible from Rome and to Italian bishops.

Eucharistic issues were raised at the first group of sessions, defined in the second, and further defined and regulated in the third. From the first the Council was determined to proceed with the definition of doctrine and the reform of abuses as distinct subjects, but at the same time. On eucharistic doctrine the real presence and transubstantiation were considered in 1546–7 and again in 1551–2, when the definitions were actually framed. Communion in bread and cup and the eucharistic sacrifice were postponed until 1562–3, but the issue of sacrifice was certainly in the minds of those who considered the real presence in 1545–52. It was postponed, because it presented the greatest difficulties to Erasmians as well as Protestants. The postponement was unfortunate, in that by the time it came to be considered, any hope of agreement between Protestants and Catholics was so remote that there was no longer any sufficient motive for condemning extravagant statements that had once been common in popular preaching. That their importance had been exaggerated in controversy is certain, but practices based upon them were recognized as superstitious and in need of reform. The condemnation of their basis in exaggerated ideas of the separate worth of each individual Mass, and of special kinds of Masses arranged in an order or orders of succession, might have averted the return of these ideas in more sophisticated forms in controversy with Protestants after the work of definition had been completed.

In 1545–52 the real presence appeared to be less controversial than transubstantiation. Those who wished to avoid the use of the latter term were still hopeful of finding common ground with Lutherans against the Swiss and their south German followers and associates. No one seriously thought of an alliance with any of these against the Lutherans. That this was intellectually conceivable is seen in a proposal supported by a single bishop in May 1547 to speak of a *conversio sacramentalis* in the definition of transubstantiation instead of a "unique and wonderful changing" of the whole substance of the bread. This would have emphasized resemblances between the eucharist and the other sacraments, especially baptism, and might have conciliated those who believed that in baptism a real sacramental gift is given, but hesitated to affirm a difference in kind between the presence of Christ in this, and in the whole action of the eucharist, and his particular presence after the consecration in what is received in communion. Cranmer, and on occasions Calvin, could use the language of substance of the real presence. Their difference from Luther related rather to what is called "oral manducation", the "pressing with the teeth" of the body and blood of Christ, and to what happens when the wicked receive this to their hurt.

A doctrine of the real presence limited to the ground common to Catholics and

Lutherans might on the one hand have been open to the objections brought by Innocent III and others, that "oral manducation" can only refer to the *species,* not the impassible body of Christ, and on the other to the possibility of reduction to a wholly spiritual presence under a figure or veil of bread. The merit of the word transubstantiation is to insist that something happens to the bread, in the final definition that "through the consecration of bread and wine a conversion is made of the whole substance of the bread into the substance of the body of Christ, and of the whole substance of the wine into the substance of his blood". Given the conviction common to all parties at the time that sacrifice, as distinct from oblation, involves change in the offering, the alternative to the transubstantiation of the bread was the transfiguration of Christ under forms of bread and wine. This line of thinking led to theologies of the eucharistic sacrifice in which Christ himself is, in a peculiar sense, slain every time the bread and wine are consecrated, in every Mass. These, as we shall see, are no longer favoured. They were never actually implied in the Tridentine definition of sacrifice in the eucharist, but they could be read out of it by those who would defend against Protestants the glory, wonder and greatness of the sacrifice of the Mass.

The definition itself may be called a conflation of four approaches. The first is concerned with the institution of a priesthood for all mankind "after the order of Melchisedech", free from the limitations of the Levitical and all other national ordinances. Christ at the Last Supper made his apostles priests of the new covenant. He inaugurated a new Passover in celebration of the old "that the assembly of the children of Israel sacrificed in memory of their exodus from Egypt". In this he would "be sacrificed by his Church through priests under visible signs, in memory of his transit from this world to the Father".

In the next paragraph this is identified with the pure offering foretold by the prophet Malachi (1 : 11), to be offered in every place as well as in Jerusalem. St. Paul pointed to this when he said it was impossible for those polluted by participation in the table of demons to be partakers of the Lord's table, meaning by table an altar in both places. "For this indeed is what was figured in similitudes through the variety of sacrifices in the time of nature and of the Law, that all good things signified by these should be included in the consummation and perfection of them all".

In the next paragraph the synod teaches "that in this divine sacrifice, celebrated in the Mass, the same Christ is contained and sacrificed bloodlessly, who on the altar of the cross offered himself once in the shedding of his blood". "This is indeed truly propitiatory, and has this effect, that if in contrition and penitence we approach God with a sincere heart and with true faith, in fear and reverence, 'we obtain mercy and find grace for our aid in need'." "One and the same victim, who offered himself on the cross is now offered by the ministry of priests, but only the manner of offering is different. The fruits of the oblation in blood are received abundantly through the unbloody offering. The one is in no way diminished by the other. It is offered for the living and for the dead who are not yet fully cleansed, in accordance with the tradition of the apostles."

The word for sacrifice here is *immolare (immolandum, incruente immolatur)*. This word is so used in pagan and Christian literature. How it is construed depends on definitions of sacrifice, then and now, but "a bloodless immolation" is not naturally read as implying the infliction of any new suffering on Christ. The difficulty in controversy arises from the insistence in the canons that follow, first that the Mass is a true and proper sacrifice, offered to God and not just to us for us to eat, and secondly that the apostles were ordained priests, that they and other priests might offer the body and blood of Christ. In the third canon it is laid down that the Mass is not only a sacrifice of praise and thanksgiving, or "a naked commemoration of the sacrifice finished on the cross", and that it is propitiatory, and not profitable only for the communicants, that it ought to be offered for the living and the dead. In the final profession of faith at the conclusion of the Council the Mass is declared to be "a true, proper and propitiatory sacrifice for the living and the dead".

All these summaries are to be understood in terms of the detailed definition, but they were often attacked, and too often defended, as if what must be at stake is the efficacy and worth of every Mass. That the Mass depends on the cross was made clear, but there was too much concentration upon errors in one direction, denying sacrifice in the Mass, and not in the other, implying a different sacrifice.

The matter of communion in the cup also called for doctrinal definition, closely linked as it is with the communion of infants and young children. This was considered before the sacrifice of the Mass, and defined on July 16, 1562, with notable moderation. Communion in the cup and the communion of infants was not indeed forbidden. In Eastern Churches in communion with Rome it has never ceased, and at this time it was widely practised in Bohemia and in parts of Germany, where it was regarded as a way of meeting the reasonable demands of moderate Reformers. The definitions and canons were directed against those who denied that Christ is received whole and entire under the *species* of bread, and affirmed that communion in bread and cup must be given to all communicants always in order to fulfil the command of Christ. Baptized children, it is said, are not bound to communicate in the eucharist in order to complete their baptism. Infant communion after baptism and confirmation had always continued in some places and on some occasions in the West as well as in the East. At the time of the Council of Trent it was going out of use, but the custom of bringing children to the Easter Vigil for baptism, confirmation and communion had not entirely ceased, and was still remembered where it had become obsolete. The occasion was taken to insist on the power of the Church to make changes in the eucharistic rite and in the use of the other sacraments.

The Reform of the Mass

On the day of the definition of the eucharistic sacrifice, September 17, 1562, a decree was passed for the reform of abuses in the Mass. This was only intended to cover the most obvious and urgent scandals. A much more comprehensive list, drawn up in August, from which these were selected, provided agenda for the reform of the missal after the conclusion of the Council. The first necessity is said in this list to be uniformity not only in rites but in ceremonies, that everywhere the Church should speak with the same voice and do the same thing. The text of the Mass required attention. Many missals had too many proper prefaces, containing untrue statements about St. Jerome and St. Augustine, and praising saints like St. Christopher and St. Roch, who if they ever existed have never been properly canonized. The offertory prayers and signs of the cross made over the oblations after the consecration are inconsistent with the view that this is completed at the words of institution. The commingling of the bread and the cup gave a handle to those who held that communion in one kind, in the consecrated wafer, is only half-communion.

A large number of complaints refer to votive Masses, especially to those celebrated with a determined number of candles. The Mass of St. Sophia and the Mass for the seven gifts of the Spirit required seven, the Mass of the apostles twelve. Masses of the rosary and for the aid of the Blessed Virgin needed tender handling, since many were devoted to them, but there was need to emphasize not the number or nature of a particular Mass, but rather that every Mass should be celebrated with the like devotion to God and love for the living and the dead. It was a scandal when a priest received alms for several Masses and then celebrated only one, but the quest for stipends, looking out for offerings in payment for Masses, was itself a scandal and had done the Church no small harm. Votive Masses for special intentions ought not to interfere with the Mass for the day. Their multiplication had cheapened the Mass. They ought not to be said without two candles on the altar and two to hear them, of which one should be the server, a tonsured clerk properly vested in surplice or cotta. Those who minister as deacons ought not to serve two or three Masses at the same time. Provision should be made for the situation when legacies for Masses are not sufficient to maintain a priest, so that prayers could be offered for those who left them in other circumstances.

A third set of complaints refer to histrionic and extravagant ceremonial gestures, especially at the elevations, and also in beating the breast in penitence. At the elevation of the host some saluted members of the congregation, others got the consecrated wafer entangled in their hair, or did not look up at their fingers as they held a chalice in peril of being spilt. Some elevate again at the end of the canon, before the Lord's Prayer. Some left the altar before the end of Mass, or near the beginning to fetch what they have forgotten to bring. All kinds of unsavoury objects were hung around altars, such as arms and armour, written and printed notices. Lights were carried round by servers while the priest at the altar was left in darkness. Music was often more refreshing to the ear than to the mind, exciting more desire than devotion. Battle and hunting songs were sung. Every kind of misbehaviour was common in church, where people brought hawks, falcons and dogs, and priests chatted in vestments, and left their birettas and gloves on the altar. Many in mortal sin celebrated without confession, and some without authority twice on the same day. Mass was celebrated in strange places, at the corners of streets and after midnight feasts, especially after weddings in the bridal chamber, after the bride and groom have gone to bed, or at funerals with putrefying bodies around. Consideration should be given to the idea that at cathedral and conventual Masses some of the ministers should communicate with the celebrant, and that the parish Mass could be made an occasion for instruction in the faith.

This was far too large an agenda for the Council to consider in their final group of sessions. The actual decree on reformation of abuses was limited to three points. Avarice is a great evil. In new foundations for the celebration of Mass everything possible should be done to avoid any suggestion of seeking after filthy lucre. Irreverence is an evil, and so care should be taken to prevent wandering, unknown priests from celebrating without licence and in private houses and other places outside the church and "oratories dedicated to divine worship" and to banish unsuitable music. This led to much stricter regulations about the licensing of priests and of altars, although these could not in practice be enforced in places where the government was hostile to the Church, as in the British Isles where most Masses were in private houses and few Catholic priests were in regular communication with their bishops before the eighteenth century. In the matter of superstition more was enjoined than could be accomplished. The practice of saying Masses with a fixed number of candles, or a fixed number of Masses, was said to be "founded more on superstition than on true religion". These should be "utterly removed from the Church", but relics of them remained. The people were to be taught "what the precious and most heavenly fruit of the most holy sacrifice really is, and from whom it comes". But how to do this was a problem, and continued to be one through the seventeenth and eighteenth centuries.

The reform of the missal was entrusted to the Pope, who set up a commission to deal with it. His successor, Pope St. Pius V, continued the work, which resulted in the publication in 1570 of an authorized edition of the *Missale Romanum ex decreto ss. Concilii Tridentini restitutum*. Unfortunately we have no reports of the commission's proceedings. We have to judge their work by the results and by comparison with the materials available for their use. The list of abuses already given is a valuable guide to their proceedings. The most urgent problem was to control the celebration of Mass by priests of little education whose conduct frequently gave rise to concern. Hence the desire to provide them with meticulous regulations for every detail of their behaviour in church. The printed book made this possible. Missals printed before the Reformation contain a great deal of detailed regulation on ceremonial points that is never found in manuscripts, but it is unsystematic and incomplete. The rubrics for ceremonial in the Missal of 1570 were nothing if not thorough. Their interpretation was regulated by a Congregation of Rites set up by Sixtus V in 1588. Their wording was clarified and improved in a new edition published by Urban VIII in 1634. This does a great deal to explain the rapid disappearance of local rites, except in a few places. The original intention was that those who could claim more than two hundred years' of use should remain; but outside the religious orders, who had their own machinery for regulation, few local rites persisted for long. The Mozarabic Missal in its printed form lacked the two hundred years' prescription, since the Missal of Ximenez was not published until 1500. It persisted only in a few places where it could claim a long continuous history before that. In any case it required more popular response than can easily be obtained where Latin is no longer close to the common speech. In other circumstances it might have developed into something different, in Latin or Spanish, but Spain in the sixteenth century was too consciously loyal to Rome for that.

The important new element in the Tridentine Missal are the detailed directions

Frontispiece in a missal of the Augustinian Friars, when they were anxious to free themselves from association with Luther. St. Augustine is represented as the scourge of heretics by his writing. Our Lady holds, over a globe which includes America, a church modelled on additions made by Sixtus V to St. Maria Maggiore in Rome.

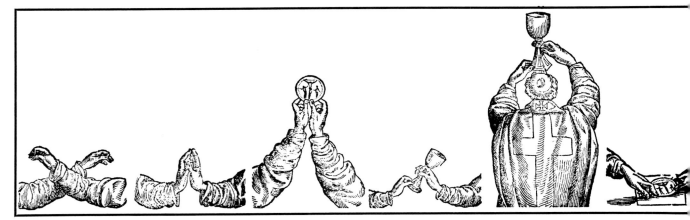

In a Dominican Missal of 1614, the gestures of consecration, fraction, commixture and communion.

for speech and ceremonies at all kinds of Masses. The significance of these is not easy for the general reader to grasp out of their context, and they will be dealt with only in relation to changes in the text. But one general remark may be made, which is relevant to a wider series of problems. The magic of the Middle Ages, in the sense of rites considered to have some automatic effect in themselves apart from prayer, was generally a consequence of the private enterprise of ecclesiastics or of ecclesiastical and conventual groups who promoted particular devotions. The authorities of the Church might be blamed for conniving at them, or profiting by them; and in a limited number of cases, mostly concerned with indulgences, for promoting attitudes that were bound to lead the simple into misbelief that this or that form of words had an automatic effect. But the rubrics of the missal were official and enforced. If uniformity had been actually achieved it could have led to the common acceptance of the belief that the proper performance of the ceremonies is on the same level as the celebration of the Mass and of the other sacraments. The Church was delivered from this by the missions in England and Protestant countries, and overseas, where strict ceremonial uniformity was impossible. Even the contentions of the missionaries, as in the matter of adaptations to the civilizations of China and India, and the preservation of local traditions by supporters of the old religion in England, Scotland and Ireland, who often resented the innovations of the Jesuits, served to underline the impossibility of a monolithic Latin Catholicism, and to call attention to the survival of Eastern Churches in communion with Rome who had liturgies of their own. Some of these were in an ambiguous position where the lines between unity and schism were hard to draw. While interest in this problem was limited by the difficulties of access to Christians in Russia and Turkey, it is never entirely absent from the consideration of liturgical questions in controversy between Catholics and Protestants.

Music in the early editions of the Missal as reformed by Pius V, in the preface of the Holy Trinity.

The Order of Mass

What the new Roman Missal did was to fix such matters as the order to be used in putting on the vestments, the use and disuse of the psalm in the preparation of priest and servers, the forms of confession and absolution in this preparation; the use of the *Gloria in excelsis* on festal days, but not at votive Masses (with stated exceptions),

and always in the standard form, without any interpolations in honour of Our Lady; the use of the creed on Sundays and on a number of specified feast days, including those of the Doctors of the Church. The Greek Doctors, St. Athanasius, St. Basil, St. Gregory Nazianzen and St. John Chrysostom, appear for the first time in the Roman calendar with the honours given to St. Ambrose, St. Jerome, St. Augustine and St. Gregory the Great.

The offertory prayers are prescribed in the form found in the first printed edition of the Roman Missal in 1474. They are found elsewhere in a variety of forms, but not in the Roman *Ordines,* and they had been criticized at the Council. They had found their way into the pope's own Mass, and despite objections they were retained. To remove references to "the immaculate victim" and "the chalice of salvation" would have raised questions about the meaning of other words and gestures in the later part of the canon that cannot easily be reconciled with the theory that consecration is completed at the words of institution. Gestures of blessing remained at the mention of "a holy sacrifice, an immaculate victim", offered by the high priest of Jerusalem in the days of Abraham, although this could be and often was construed as referring to the consecrated host and chalice. The one change in the text that must be regarded as a direct result of controversy was at the commingling of the bread with the cup after the breaking of the bread.

This, as we have already seen, had a long and curious history. The rite of the *fermentum,* in which a fragment specially sent from the pope's Mass was dropped into the chalice, was originally peculiar to the churches served by presbyters in Rome itself and not in the country round it. There it was done after the Lord's Prayer, at the sign of peace, at any rate after St. Gregory the Great moved the Lord's Prayer to the end of the canon, and so away from the fraction and the communion. But in every Mass, including the pope's own, another commingling followed the fraction in the rites of immediate preparation for the communion. This second commingling in the Roman rite was originally connected with the preparation of one or more supplementary chalices for the communion of the faithful. Since it was not considered convenient or suitable to consecrate two or more chalices together, these were blessed either by mingling the blood of Christ with wine that had not yet been consecrated, or by dropping into such wine a fragment of the consecrated host. It may well be that this was the original place and function of the *fermentum* when the Peace was more closely connected with the fraction.

When Roman orders were used in places where the custom of the *fermentum* was not understood, either the fraction must be anticipated, or the commingling postponed until after it. As things worked out a formula came to be used that really belonged to the blessing of supplementary chalices, but used at an earlier point, just after the Peace, where the *fermentum* had been dropped into the cup. In the English rites of Salisbury, Bangor, York and Hereford, and no doubt elsewhere in the north of Europe, this was done after the *Agnus Dei*, "O Lamb of God . . .", and in a form that was acceptable to the revisers of the Roman Missal: "*Haec sacrosancta commixtio corporis et sanguinis Domini nostri Jesu Christi fiat mihi et omnibus sumentibus* [all who take] *salus mentis et corporis. . . .*" In these rites the Peace was doubled, before the commingling and again after it. The new Roman Missal avoided this but altered the older Roman form in the Missal of 1474: "*Fiat commixtio et consecratio corporis et sanguinis domini nostri Jesu Christi: Accipientibus nobis vitam eternam Amen.*" This was after the fraction and the Peace, but before the *Agnus Dei*, where it remained in the new missal, but in the form "*Haec commixtio & consecratio. . . .*"

This clearly belongs to the consecration of chalices for the people's communion. More evidently than the English form it is a consecration, for Roman conservatism reduced revision to a minimum.

Seasons and Saints

The same conservatism was shown with regard to the peculiar uses of certain seasons, of the three Masses of Christmas, and of passiontide, where ancient forms lingered whose origins were at this time imperfectly understood, such as the Mass of the pre-sanctified on Good Friday and the Easter Vigil, at this time generally celebrated on Holy Saturday early in the day. Directions for these were found in all the Roman *Ordines* and had already been to some extent adapted to the needs of places outside Rome. At one point, however, the Tridentine rubrics betray the needs of controversy in that at the Mass of the pre-sanctified the wine and water poured into the chalice is not to be blessed and is not considered to have been consecrated by commingling with a fragment of the consecrated host, which is silently dropped in. No sign of peace is given, and no *Agnus Dei* spoken. Communion continued to be given on Good Friday in many places in the seventeenth century, but it is significant that in Russia, where Latin theological influence was most potent *after* the Council of Trent, children are not communicated in the liturgy of the pre-sanctified, which may be used on any day when the full liturgy is not allowed. In Greece and the Middle East, when the same Byzantine liturgy is used under like circumstances, the cup is considered to be consecrated by contact, and children communicated as on any other day.

In the matter of saints' days, the aim of the editors was to reduce the burden of new feasts by a return to those found in Roman calendars of the eleventh century, with a few later additions, mostly of Italian saints such as St. Francis, St. Clare and St. Catherine of Siena. St. Dominic and St. Bridget of Sweden were also included,

Frontispiece of a book on the ceremonial of a papal Mass, published in 1610, with an impression of the Pope presiding from a throne in the apse as in early times.

High Mass in Picart's illustrations of the ceremonies of all religions (1725).

but the only German, St. Ursula, was a legendary martyr connected with a cemetery at Cologne, identified as the burial place of the saint and her thousand companions, all virgins. A common of saints provided texts for the vigil of the feast of an apostle, for a bishop and martyr, a martyr not a bishop, a martyr in Eastertide, for confessors who were and were not bishops, for virgins who were and were not martyrs, for a lady martyr who was not a virgin, and finally for a lady who was neither a virgin nor a martyr. This helped to eliminate the extravagances that are often found in Mozarabic Masses in honour of saints, and were doubtless common in diocesan rites in the Middle Ages, and for the time being to increase considerably the number of days that were free of feasts, 150 in round numbers, if octaves are not included. But new canonizations soon filled up the gaps, and some of the feasts eliminated found their way back again.

Occasional Masses

These are at the end of the missal, beginning with the Mass on the anniversary of the dedication of a church, followed by votive Masses of the Holy Trinity, of the angels, and of St. Peter and St. Paul. Masses of the Holy Spirit, of the Blessed Sacrament, and of the Cross and of the Passion of Christ precede a series of votive Masses of the Blessed Virgin at various times in the year, in Advent, in Christmastide, between Christmastide and Easter, in Eastertide and after Pentecost. A whole series of Masses for particular needs, at the time of a papal election, for the anniversary of a bishop's consecration, for the healing of schism, for victory and peace, for the sick, for travellers, and at a nuptial Mass, precede the series of Masses for the dead. There are Masses "against the pagans", presumably Turks, and "in any necessity". There are also a number of collects which may be inserted in the Mass of the day, except on feasts that have the rank of doubles. The causes for which prayers, but not particular votive Masses, are provided, include concord in the congregation, the need for rain or sunshine, diseases of animals, public penitents, enemies, captives, prisoners of war, and those in peril at sea. There are also prayers for the priest to say for himself at his own Mass, for the gift of tears, against evil thoughts, and for continence, humility, patience and charity, for others who are tempted and troubled, for great friends, for enemies, and for the living and the dead.

The regulations concerning the saying and singing of votive Masses are clearly intended to prevent them displacing the Mass of the day, except on certain days without any other celebration where a sung requiem or other votive Mass may be in order, and in the case of Masses of Our Lady on any Saturday outside Lent and the Ember Seasons where no double or semi-double feast is actually kept on the day. This must have made it much more difficult to continue the celebration of votive Masses in a series for seven or thirty days for a particular end. This had been common in the Middle Ages, especially in connection with Masses for the dead where a "Gregorian" series of seven or thirty was supposed to be an infallible way of getting a soul out of purgatory. These persisted, but generally on privileged altars where no other Mass was said, and therefore the series might be deemed to continue after interruption for a day or two. The Mass of St. Sophia with the seven candles, and Mass for the seven gifts of the Holy Spirit, disappeared from the books, like the Mass of St. Amatorius, whose identity baffles historians of the Council of Trent. The idea that some rituals are more potent than others by no means disappeared, but it came to be annexed to a proper conformity with the decrees of the Sacred Congregation of Rites, who were at any rate on the alert to avoid new scandals, if they thought more harm than good would come from the extirpation of old ones, denounced by the reformers. Severity there could only draw attention to the element of truth in their charges.

The requiem Masses in the missal, selected from a wider variety to be found in the earlier printed texts and manuscripts, are all coloured by the attitude to the dead that had become characteristic of the Latin West in the age of the Cluniacs, in the tenth and eleventh centuries. Objections were made at the Council to the offertory anthem common to all of them, that to speak of deliverance "from the pains of hell" and "from the mouth of the lion", might be taken to imply a possibility of salvation from the jaws of hell after the death of the body. If this had been reformed the loophole would have been closed. In the controversies of the Reformation both

sides were convinced that it was dangerous to attenuate the risks or the pains of eternal damnation.

Varieties of Masses

Despite all this uniformity new kinds of variation appeared. They are foreshadowed by the attempt of John Burckard (or Burchard), a papal master of ceremonies before the Reformation, to regulate the behaviour of those who attend Mass. His *Ordo Missae,* first published in 1502 and in a number of editions later, was much used by the framers of rubrics, but they did not attempt as he had done to lay down rules for the congregation. According to these, at a said Mass they should kneel from beginning to end except at the gospel, when they should stand to attention. At a Mass that is sung on a Sunday or feast, or on any ordinary weekday between Easter and the Feast of the Holy Trinity, at the end of the Octave of Pentecost, they should kneel for the confession at the beginning, and then stand until the elevation of the host, when they should kneel to adore and afterwards rise again and remain standing until the end. But if Mass is sung for the dead or on a day that is not a feast and not in Eastertide, they should kneel longer at the beginning, in Lent until just before the gospel, and kneel again from the time when the celebrant says the *sanctus* until the end of the Mass. Otherwise, unless they have the opportunity to sit, they should stand. Seats were a new feature but becoming more common. By way of an afterthought Burchard notes a number of places where sitting at a sung Mass could be permitted, before the gospel, after the creed and before and after the offertory anthem until the priest begins the preface at "Lift up your hearts", and again before the dismissals at the end. He also notes the times for bending the knee in the creed, the gospel for the epiphany, and the "last gospel" from St. John at the end of the Mass.

Few in his time expected the congregation to pay more attention to what the priest was doing than to their own prayers, but Burchard's emphasis on the distinction between a sung and a said Mass points to the shape of things to come. At the Council of Trent the low Mass of the chantry priest was the heart of the problem. He must be made at any rate to do and to say everything if any confidence is to be restored in the efficacy of the Church's offering. So low Mass is assumed as normal. High Masses are limited to places where qualified deacons, subdeacons and other ministers are available. It is no longer enough to make do with young clerks, only just tonsured, to perform such offices at the parish Mass. Thus high Mass comes to be limited to cathedral and conventual churches, and there not necessarily used on ordinary Sundays. But sung Mass allowed of other kinds of elaboration. Polyphonic music had been criticized at the Council by those who were loyal to Gregorian chant, but it had not been forbidden, and it was in fact on the way to new and important developments in the years that followed. The singing of hymns at Mass had long been common in Germany, and developed further in the period after the Council, a period of Catholic renewal and revival in German lands, and of the composition of great *chorales* by German Protestants. At sung Masses in Germany chants in German of a like sort sometimes replaced the gradual and the offertory anthem. They were frequently sung at the beginning of the Mass and during the communion.

Opposite: Infant communion in Cyprus: the child's distress embarrasses his elder sister and shocks his grandmother, but not his mother.

Frequent Communion

In earlier places in the present volume reference has frequently been made to be absence of lay communicants from the Mass in most places right through the Middle Ages from the sixth to the sixteenth century. The causes of this are complex, and it may not have been so complete as is generally thought. In the case of St. Catharine of Genoa it is clear that in an Italian city at the end of the fifteenth century a married woman with children could make her communion regularly for some time without going to confession at all, before there was any scandal. This would not have happened if some good wives and mothers had not always been accustomed to make their communions often.

It was in the seventeenth century that an increase in the number of these, and of laymen "making their souls" under spiritual direction from Jesuits and others, gave rise to controversy. In most parts of Western Europe through most of the Middle Ages it would be fair to say that the laity were treated as penitents in Lent, absolved at Easter, who fell back into sin immediately after and had to go through the same again next year. The Protestant solution accepted and exaggerated the pessimistic view of the human condition found in the anti-Pelagian writings of St. Augustine, and in St. Bernard and other ascetics of the Middle Ages, but found an answer in free forgiveness, in a grace that is imputed, not imparted, and so cannot be measured by its fruits, although fruits are to be expected. This could produce confidence, courage and holiness, but also doubt and depression among those uncertain of their salvation. St. Francis de Sales and others in the Catholic Reformation took a more tender view of the plight of human nature, derived at least in part from the Greek Fathers by way of Erasmus. Their practice in regard to absolution and holy communion brought them criticism not only from Protestants but from old-fashioned Catholics. What was and is called Jansenism has much less to do with Calvinist influences than many Catholics at the time supposed and some still think. The common ground between Catholic and Protestant Augustinians in France, England and the Netherlands is part of a common inheritance from Catholic belief and practice.

St. Francis de Sales, and those Jesuits who encouraged frequent communion, were in their day making an innovation, though they too appealed to St. Augustine and to other earlier authorities. Some Dutch Protestants and more Anglicans agreed with them. They were called Arminians by strict Calvinists, who detected in a Dutch theologian with the name of Hermann, and in some Cambridge men, a dangerous tendency to defend the freedom of the will after the manner of Erasmus. The practical effect of this was greater among Catholics than among Anglicans or Protestants, in that the number of laymen and women who made their communions often increased to a notable extent. But many Catholics made their communions outside the Mass. In the seventeenth century, as in the twentieth, frequent communion led to the renewal of liturgy. But it began and made progress without it, and there is always a possibility of conflict between the idea of common participation in the Mass, and the idea of the Mass as primarily a way of consecrating the host for adoration and communion.

IX Early Liturgical Movements

Gallican Scholarship

Liturgical studies, as we have seen, had a limited role in the controversies of the Reformation. Western scholars were aware of the existence of Eastern liturgies, but only a few specialists studied them. The editions printed in Venice for use in the Venetian dominions were naturally an object of Protestant suspicions, since those who printed them, and many of those who used them, lived under subjection to Catholic authorities. Most of the copies went down the Adriatic and were sold in Constantinople or Greece. The Mozarabic Missal received more attention, and manuscripts found in monastic libraries were sometimes cited to prove that the Roman rite in its modern form was not so old as the Church supposed, but they were not effective arguments for the theology of the Reformation. Catholics who used them in controversy sometimes accepted uncritically the dates given to them by their Protestant opponents, but they hesitated to print more material of the same kind, and very little material from early Gallican rites was available in print before 1671.

The turning-point came with the publication in that year of a book on the history of the Mass by Cardinal Bona, and in 1680 of materials for the study of early Roman and Gallican liturgy in the Roman libraries, where Bona had used them, by another learned Italian cardinal, Giuseppe-Maria Tommasi (otherwide called Thomasius, 1649–1713). In 1685 Jean Mabillon, A French Benedictine of the Congregation of St. Maur, published his definitive *De Liturgia Gallicana Libri III*. By this time more Eastern material had become available in Jacob Goar's *Euchologion,* published in 1647 as a liturgical contribution to a great French

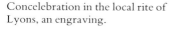
Concelebration in the local rite of Lyons, an engraving.

collection of Byzantine historical material. The golden age of liturgical scholarship followed Mabillon's *Liturgia Gallicana* and his *Museum Italicum* (1687), with more diverse material. These studies were international and interdenominational. The papers of John Ernst Gräbe, a Prussian Lutheran who became an Anglican deacon, living in Oxford and London from 1695 to 1711, when he was run over by a stage-coach, are now in the Bodleian Library at Oxford. They contain letters from Catholic, Lutheran, Reformed and Eastern Orthodox scholars in many parts of Europe relating to the study of the Fathers, and especially to questions bearing on early liturgy, which was one of Gräbe's special subjects. Among his friends were Edward Stephens, an Anglican priest who adapted the liturgy in the eighth book of the *Apostolic Constitutions* to his purposes, and died in communion with the Orthodox East; William Whiston, who made extravagant claims for the doctrinal and liturgical authority of the *Apostolic Constitutions,* which Gräbe was at pains to refute; Bishop Archibald Campbell, who was one of those primarily responsible for the liturgy of the Non-jurors; and Thomas Hearne, the Oxford antiquary. Thomas Brett, another Nonjuring bishop, who belonged to the same circle, produced the first English translations of early and Eastern liturgical materials in 1718.

These dates are important. By this time Eugene Renaudot had published nearly all the Eastern liturgies, and Dom Edmund Martène his *De Antiquis Ecclesiae Ritibus* (1700–02). More was to come in the middle of the eighteenth century, but standards of liturgical scholarship were established by 1720, as the relevance of the East to Western developments became plain. Very little of this material was available at the time of the Reformation, or in the controversies that immediately followed. It began to be used practically in the eighteenth century.

Offertory procession in Mass for the dead at the end of the seventeenth century; a French survival.

Gallican Liturgical Movements

Some of the French dioceses had rites of their own which survived the Tridentine reform. The position of the diocesan rites had been weakened by the religious wars, in which many books had been lost or burnt. The new Roman Breviary and Missal were cheap, and had to be allowed in dioceses which maintained their claims to their own uses. But the differences had little or no real religious or theological significance. The matter would not have been important if the growth of scholarship had not led some French dioceses to revise their breviaries, and even their missals, on lines which, in the eyes of the religious orders and other strong partisans of the prerogatives of the papacy, betrayed an alarming tendency to play down St. Peter, the Blessed Virgin, and any traditions not adequately supported by Scripture and sufficient historical evidence. This went further, where the missals were concerned, when the original Gallican liturgy was discovered, as distinct from local uses in the later Middle Ages. Many people started looking for relics of this in a spirit of devout antiquarianism, but they often seemed to be more interested in reviving quaint superstitions than in deepening devotion.

But some of them did anticipate modern developments. The experiments of Jube, the parish priest at Asnières, on the west bank of the Seine, not far from Paris, are described by Père Louis Bouyer in *Liturgical Piety*. He never used the high altar in his church except on Sundays and feasts when he had a congregation. He had no lights or cross on the altar, except the processional cross and the tapers, carried in and put in position when the Mass began. He involved everyone in the preparation, in the psalm and the confession and absolution, and after singing the collect sat down and listened to the other ministers singing the epistle and gospel. He had an offertory procession with offerings of all kinds, and blessed some of them at the end of the canon. He never began the canon before the choir had finished the *sanctus* and *benedictus qui venit*, and always said it loud enough for everyone in his small church to hear him. For this reason the devotees of rubrics regarded him with dismay. He was classed with those who wanted to get rid of rosaries and benediction, and with the Jansenists who wished to restore primitive penitential discipline. But there is no evidence that he was a Jansenist except in the sense that all critics of some of the measures taken against them incurred the charge of sympathizing with them.

One such measure was a brief of Pope Alexander VII against a French translation of the Roman Missal. This was obtained in 1661 by the French Prime Minister, Cardinal Mazarin, who misrepresented the motives of the author, Voisin, alleging that he had translated the Missal in order to celebrate Mass in French. Mazarin's object was to discredit the vicars-general of the Archbishop of Paris, Cardinal de Retz, exiled for political reasons, and to embroil them and him with the Holy See. The brief appeared to condemn all translations, especially of the canon, but it was not in fact enforced, and other translations soon appeared, not only in French. In the eighteenth century even English Roman Catholics, who had suffered so much for their loyalty to Rome, had one. Translations, however, were assailed with venom by those who identified the mystery of the Mass with a secret that must always be hidden, a language that by its very nature cannot be rightly interpreted. The difficulty of translating the Roman canon tended to confirm this view.

A cabinet used as an altar in a recusant household of the eighteenth century, now at Oscott College in the West Midlands.

The Gallican liturgists had their faults. Their Latin was learnt from the classics in good schools, and they preferred the correct Latin verse of their own hymns to the low Latin of the Breviary. They were impatient with mediaeval and modern devotions and with any authority other than antiquity. But it is not a fault to prefer Scripture to the overgrowth of legend, the psalms to most of the hymns, and in an age when historical consciousness was gradually growing, to have desired discrimination between history and fable. Pope Benedict XIV in the middle of the eighteenth century certainly contemplated the revision of the Roman Breviary on similar lines. After the French Revolution the Gallican missals and breviaries became curiosities, collector's pieces, but they survived in libraries and were used in the modern revision of the office under St. Pius X at the beginning of this century. Gallicanism at that time was a dirty word, and no acknowledgements were made. Today it is prudent to express sympathy with those who printed the Amens in the canon in a way that implied that they should be said by the congregation, and therefore that the prayers might be heard, and the rubrics so that the celebrant was not obliged to recite at a high Mass everything sung or said by the choir and the other ministers, as if it were a low Mass of his own.

Something should be said of German developments which began later and lasted longer into "the Age of Reason", the eighteenth century, when a kind of "Catholic classicism" sought to take over bodily liturgical forms from primitive Christianity. Demands were made, and sometimes met, for a single parish Mass on Sundays, with a sermon after the gospel, communion in the Mass, a reduction in instrumental music, and a development of popular singing and even of common prayer in German on the lines of the priest's prayer, not in the same words, but at the same time. The offertory procession, the kiss of peace, and concelebration by several priests of the same Mass were also proposed as desirable aims. Some dissatisfaction was expressed with the use of the rosary at Mass. In some places this seems to have been sung. Perhaps the most permanent consequence of this movement were German versions of the *Gloria in excelsis, sanctus, Agnus Dei* and other parts of the "ordinary" of the Mass, which continued in use, so far as the choir and congregation were concerned, at high Masses and sung Masses in many parts of north Germany through the nineteenth century, and so prepared the way for the German Mass of today.

But in Germany as in France the cause of reform suffered through association with other movements, some of them rationalist, some directed against the papacy and the Jesuits, and toward a union of German Catholics and Protestants against Rome, especially at the time of the Emperor Joseph II and other "enlightened despots", Frederick II of Prussia and Catharine II of Russia, immediately before the French Revolution. The Synod of Pistoia in Tuscany in 1786 adopted a series of fifty-seven articles proposed to it by Joseph II's brother, the Archduke Leopold, who succeeded Joseph in 1790 as the Emperor Leopold II. These covered a wide range of questions, from predestination to the precedence of parish priests over canons at diocesan synods. In passing they propose vernacular liturgies and abolition of the cult of the sacred heart and of "images". What this meant in practice was shortly shown by the removal of mantles from madonnas. The Italian poor showed what they thought of it by a riot, when they broke into the palace of Scipio Ricci, the principal episcopal protagonist of the reforms, and burnt his books. When Leopold left for Austria he lost police protection and had to resign his see.

The French Revolution divided the future from the past, more decisively in France, Belgium and Italy than the Industrial Revolution in Great Britain at about the same time. In France it was fatal to the special "liberties of the Gallican Church" in regard to Rome, for these had always been associated with an alliance of crown and altar. Gallicanism was further weakened by the Concordat of 1801, when Pope Pius VII suppressed all the French sees. If the bishops did not resign, they were

This tiny chalice and paten, easily hidden, are preserved at Oscott.

This thurible bears the date of 1709. It was made for use in the English missions when small articles, easily concealed, were essential. It could be used for incense but also for hot water to warm the priest's hands.

English Roman Catholics began to build their own churches again at the end of the eighteenth century. St. Benet's, Liverpool, still has the air of 1793.

deposed. A few of them went into schism, and set up a "petite église". The object of this was to make up a new map of dioceses and to appoint new bishops in concert with the government of the French Republic. The author of the concordat, Napoleon Bonaparte, sought as First Consul and as Emperor of the French to protect "the Gallican liberties". But he had destroyed their basis in the history of French dioceses. Henceforth the French clergy depended on the government for their salaries, until the separation of Church and State a hundred years afterward, but priests more and more looked to the Pope to protect them from the State and the bishops.

Romantic Ultramontanism

The romantic revival of interest in the Middle Ages found ecclesiastical expression in England through the Oxford Movement, Anglican Ritualism, and the "second spring" of English Catholicism; in Catholic Europe in the kind of enthusiasm for the mediaeval past expressed by Chateaubriand in his *Genie de Christianisme*, by Montalembert, in his book on *The Monks of the West,* by Lammenais, Lacordaire, Bonald and other traditionalists, and finally by Dom Prosper Guéranger, the founder and first Abbot of Solesmes, the Benedictine abbey that became a great centre for Gregorian chant in the 1830s. The Benedictines of the nineteenth century loved the liturgy and did much to promote its careful, prayerful performance, and the spiritual understanding of the texts. They knew that it had a history, but they were more aware of complexity in the history of the office than of the Mass. They saw this history as beginning with a common apostolic tradition, and returning to uniformity with the diffusion of the Roman rite. They saw it as a glory that

German and French Benedictines and Cistercians took the Latin office as it stood to Africa, and sang it with full solemnity there.

They knew the Eastern rites, but as practical obstacles to the effective union of Eastern Churches with Rome, and saw the separated Churches of the East, and all that had come from the Reformation, as simply deviations from one true Church of Christ. In the study of liturgical texts they were strangely indifferent, not indeed to history, but to historical questions, and they had no desire to bring the laity to a more active participation in the life of the Church. They wished them to be, as they had been in the Middle Ages, spectators of liturgical splendours.

In the course of time, however, there came to be monks at Solesmes who knew a good deal about history. Dom Paul Cagin, originally an expert on the history of church music, began at the end of the nineteenth century to apply to the Roman canon some of the methods of higher criticism, with thoroughness and an engaging charm. His conclusions had something in common with those reached through a different application of the same methods by Dom R. H. Connolly of Downside Abbey, his friend Edmund Bishop, and the German scholar Edward Schwartz, that the eucharistic prayer of a new bishop in the Latin and Ethiopian versions of what was beginning to be called *The Egyptian Church Order* depends on an original older than other eucharistic prayers related to it. But while Dom Cagin called it *"Ap."* for Apostolic, Schwartz and Dom Connolly, supported by Edmund Bishop, assigned it to Hippolytus in Rome about 217.

Dom Cagin was following the lines laid down by Ferdinand Probst, who in 1870 revived the theory held by Whiston and others in the seventeenth century, that the liturgy in the eighth book of the *Apostolic Constitutions* is substantially "Clementine", a text of the first or the early second century, current in Rome and everywhere else. In a form modified by a German Lutheran, Dr. Paul Drews, this was accepted substantially by Father Adrian Fortescue in *The Mass, a Study of the Roman Liturgy* (1912), a standard handbook for English-speaking Catholics and many Anglicans before and after World War I. Fortescue could not agree with Dom Cagin that an older version of the Roman Mass, intermediate between the original *Ap.* and what came to be the classical text, could be reconstructed from Gallican and Mozarabic materials. They agreed, however, that the Roman canon was "dislocated", a collection of fragments from older texts with no rational order. This gave pleasure to Anglicans planning a revision of their own *Prayer Book,* who could hope to produce something impressive that might influence change in the Roman Catholic Church. Other Anglicans, however, corresponded with Edmund Bishop, who held that the Roman canon had begun to be written down in something like its present form before any serious question of eucharistic theology had been raised or the divinity of the Holy Spirit defined. The conclusions that they drew from his negative anlysis were theirs, not his. They were used to oppose the introduction of an invocation of the Spirit for the consecration of the eucharistic elements and of the communicants into a revision of the Anglican liturgy. No one at this time was proposing a revision of the Roman Missal as well as of the Breviary. But if they had, the question would have been raised by those who, like Peter of Blois in the thirteenth century, thought the Roman canon not very impressive, and not at all clear about the consecration.

Solesmes, the liturgical centre in the days of Dom Prosper Guéranger.

Augustus Pugin was a devout Catholic, but his *Contrasts* were not always favourable to his co-religionists. The altar on the left resembles the kind of reconstruction favoured by Anglican Ritualists. The one on the right is set up by enthusiasts for Italianate Baroque.

John Henry Newman drawn in the 1830s, while he was still at St. Mary's, Oxford.

Anglican Ritualism

The English revolution, in industry, not in politics, immensely enhanced the position of Protestant nonconformity in English society, and by introducing a large number of Irish labourers, soon followed by continental immigrants, many of them Italian, gave to the Catholic Church in England a much larger rank and file. It became for the most part an urban community, with a few strongholds in the countryside where Catholic gentry had always survived. Henceforth the Church of England had to struggle for her existence against powerful rivals, Catholic and Protestant. Evangelicals would have transformed it into a genteel variety of popular Protestantism, recruited from nonconformists who had come up in the world. But other elements in it, Broad as well as High, resented this and made the most of the *Prayer Book* services. There were those who wanted to make the Order of Holy Communion like the Mass as it was on the eve of the Reformation, insisting that, since the ecclesiastical laws had never been fully revised, the canons of the Church as they stood then, unless explicitly repealed, were still part of the law of the land. Ecclesiastical lawyers were indeed accustomed to invoke them in matters concerning marriages and wills. Antiquarians of this school were able to work out an English use with the aid of missals printed in the fifty years before the Reformation, and printed again with the aid of such antiquarian institutes as the the Surtees Society and the Alcuin Club. Others thought this unpractical and turned to the Roman rubrics for detailed advice in interpreting a like situation. But both had, and

used, the advantages of a liturgy in English, in which their congregations could be
involved, not only by singing hymns, but through the creed, the *sanctus,* and the
Gloria in excelsis, to which English versions of the *benedictus qui venit* and the *Agnus
Dei* were soon added, and spread into the choirs of cathedrals. In one aspect this was
part of a whole movement for the restoration of medieval monuments and the
building of new Gothic churches, which is generally embraced under the name of
"the Gothic Revival". This was much more successful in England than in Scotland
and France, and on the whole more popular with Anglicans than with Catholics.
Augustus Pugin, himself a convert to Catholicism and a protagonist of "the revival
of Christian architecture", complained of his own co-religionists that they were
allured by the pagan seductions of the Italian Renaissance, of St. Peter's at Rome,
and of the Baroque.

Agitation to put down Ritualism by Lord Shaftesbury and other Evangelicals
only hastened its diffusion. That theological leaders of the Tractarian or Oxford
Movement, and then some Ecclesiologists and Ritualists, became Roman Catholics, intensified Protestant fears, but did not destroy the movement. Differences on
liturgical questions within it developed between the Ritualists, not only over
Roman or English medieval uses, but over the possibility of improving the *Prayer
Book* by revision. This was originally an Evangelical idea, a way of "putting down
Ritualism". But bishops and moderate churchmen, Broad as well as High, came to
prefer the idea of a revised prayer book, with some concessions to Ritualism, to the
development inside the Church of England of an enclave taking all its standards of
liturgical behaviour from the latest thing in Rome.

So liturgical studies returned. In Scotland they had never died; there G. H.
Forbes, who defended the Scottish Office, the work of Nonjurors in the eighteenth
century, did valuable work on the Gallican liturgies in the middle of the nineteenth.
He and his collaborator, J. M. Neale, a Cambridge Ecclesiologist, helped to develop

Dr Pusey in old age, about 1875.

The catching of converts as seen
by Catholic schoolboys in
country woods in the 1850's, a
cartoon at Oscott.

a bias in Anglican liturgical studies in favour of what is common to Eastern and Western liturgies other than the Roman rite. This was worked out on the lines of Probst and his disciples, who thought that even the Roman rite was derived from the *Apostolic Constitutions* or similar Eastern liturgical material.

This was a liturgical movement of the study, in Oxford and Cambridge. The practical contribution of Anglo-Catholic parishes to liturgical renewal was the discovery that crowds of poor people in the East End of London, and in places like St. Barnabas', Pimlico and St. Matthew's, Westminster, could respond with enthusiasm to something very like an English version of the Roman Mass. While Anglo-Catholic priests went for holidays in Belgium to observe the proper cut of liturgical vestments, French and Belgian priests found means of inquiring into the social composition of Anglo-Catholic congregations. The best of the slum priests, in Portsmouth and other provincial towns as well as in London, were more interested in people than in incense. They shared concerns with the Belgians. They went on ministering to those who found it natural to accept the ministrations of the vicar, whatever he wore and whatever he said. Such folk were sure that they were not papists, but they had never thought of themselves as Protestants either. They did not object to being described as Catholic Christians. Those brought up in this way of worshipping now find themselves naturally at home with the new Roman Mass. They may be more at ease with it than they are with new Anglican revisions, carefully devised to please all parties in the Church of England. But those whose meticulous observation of the rubrics in the Tridentine Missal took them into the Roman Catholic Church before 1960, are less satisfied.

The process of revising the liturgy of the Church of England did not seriously get under way before 1914. The methods necessary for preparing ecclesiastical legislation that could be accepted or rejected by Parliament without prolonged debate over details were not settled until 1918. The discussion of proposals for a *Revised Prayer Book* was therefore contemporary with the beginnings of the modern Liturgical Movement in the Catholic Church. In this discussion Edmund Bishop's interpretation of the context and meaning of the Roman canon was used after his death by some of his Anglican admirers to rally "Western" Anglo-Catholics as well as Evangelical Protestants in opposition to proposals that would develop ideas of the real presence and of sacrifice in the eucharist on Eastern rather than Western lines. It would be a mistake to identify Bishop with all the arguments used. No doubt he was critical of the kind of reconstruction of primitive liturgy favoured by Dom Paul Cagin and Father Adrian Fortescue, and by some of the Anglican scholars who supported the *Revised Prayer Book*. He regarded the Eastern liturgies as theologically more developed than the Roman rite, but this does not mean that he was hostile to such developments or that he in any way shared the prejudices of Dom Gregory Dix and other Western Anglo-Catholics against Syrian ideas of "drinking the Holy Spirit", which they considered exotic and rather unpleasant. His friend Dom Connolly was a Syriac scholar, and in his collection of newspaper cuttings preserved at Downside is an article by Maurice Baring on Russian city churches in which Bishop has underlined "the smell of the poor".

X The Liturgical Movement—1909–63

Dom Lambert Beauduin (1873–1960)

The modern liturgical movement is generally considered to have begun in 1909, with an address by Dom Lambert, then a monk of Mont-César, to a Catholic conference in Malines. The address led almost immediately to the circulation of weekly sheets on the texts of the Sunday Mass for use in parishes, soon bound up into a missal for Sundays, and then to the publication of a solid review in French, *Questions liturgiques et paroissiales*, on liturgy in the parishes. Thirty years later the idea that the whole people should actively participate in liturgical worship had made considerable progress in France, Germany, Austria, Belgium, Catholic Switzerland, and elsewhere. But Dom Lambert himself was under a cloud, living in retirement at a château in Berry, exiled from the monastery of his foundation where the Byzantine and Latin rites were celebrated together, because some of "the monks of unity" had gone into schism. But the Archbishop of Bourges and the Sulpicians there were kind to him and had uses for him, and at Bourges in April 1939 he had lunch with the superior of an Anglican religious community and one of his younger brethren, the author of this book.

At this time many French churchmen sympathized with Franco's Spain and hoped for peace with Germany through an understanding with Mussolini. Later they supported Marshal Pétain. After the liberation of France they were in trouble with De Gaulle and the Resistance, which included many supporters of Dom Lambert's ideas. A friend of his in the Roman diplomatic service, sent to the Balkans, where his dangerous ways of expressing ideas could do little harm, was now sent to Paris to deal with this difficult situation. Dom Lambert ventured to call on him, and was overjoyed to hear his unmistakable voice calling "Lambert, Lambert". When Angelo Roncalli sat him down on his legatine throne, Dom Lambert was no longer out on a limb. Before very long he was able to return to his monks in their second home at Chevetogne, where they still are. There he lived to pray for the soul of Pius XII and to prophesy not only Roncalli's election as Pope John XXIII, but the significance of his reign, of which he himself had little idea as yet. Dom Lambert died in January 1960 at the age of eighty-six, less than a year after his friend had announced his intention of summoning an ecumenical council.

Prophet is the right word to describe Dom Lambert. His whole life was a kind of prophecy. He began as a secular parish priest and became a Benedictine in 1906, when the influence of Solesmes was still dominant. He had already seen that the advance of education made it possible to have a choir in every parish who could not only sing, but understand what they were singing, and lead the congregation in understanding. But to do this they must understand the liturgy, not only intellectually but spiritually. The best place to start discovering what this could mean was still a Benedictine monastery, with Dom Guéranger's *Liturgical Year* as a starting-point, since at any rate the texts were there, presented not only in Latin, but in French, English and German, and in other languages to Catholics in all nations. Dom Lambert went on to discover that in Transylvania, Syria and Palestine Catholics in communion with Rome, and Eastern Orthodox in schism, were singing the same Byzantine liturgy in competition, in vernaculars commonly understood, in Romanian and Arabic, and that this had been so elsewhere in the West as well as in the East, before the gap between liturgy and common speech widened. It was a new idea that the Eastern rites, commonly regarded as museum pieces, were relevant to parish life in the West.

In 1914 war interrupted the development of the movement, but gave Dom Lambert himself an opportunity to acquire a legendary reputation as a leader of resistance to the Germans in Belgium. It was at this time that his English contacts began to develop; but the episode is also important as a prophecy of the role of liturgical movements in resistance to Hitler in Germany and in France. Dom Lambert was already aware of an important difference between Latin North Africa, where a flourishing Christian Church became extinct in the twelfth century, and the Syrian lands from Sinai to Mesopotamia, conquered by the Muslims earlier than North Africa. These were still substantially Christian countries at the time of the Crusades. Christians in the seventeenth century were a much larger minority than they are today. They have been reduced not so much by conversion to Islam as by massacre, starvation, and emigration to other lands where the enterprise of civilized Christian Syrians is acceptable. Churches with a strong popular liturgical life have extraordinary powers of persistence, denied to those who depend too much on the education of their clergy.

This power began to be tested and perceived again after 1917, not only in the Soviet Union. Many Parisians became aware of Eastern Orthodox services held in garages with a congregation largely of taxi-drivers, who sang liturgical chants. Dom Lambert Beauduin's opportunity to help arose through his contact with Andrew Szepticky, the Metropolitan of Lvov and head of the Ukrainian Church in communion with Rome. His flock were descended from that element in the Russia of Kiev who in the conflicts between Rome and Constantinople in the Middle Ages kept a foot in both camps. Their union with Rome was consolidated when they were incorporated in Lithuania and so in Greater Poland in the days of the Catholic Reformation. But when Poland was partitioned, those who fell into the hands of Russia were pressured into unity with Moscow and schism with Rome by the Czar. Those of Galicia, under the Austrian Empire, were protected by the Austrians, always more favourable to the smaller and weaker nationalities in their possessions than to the formidable and strong. After 1918, when the Austrian Empire fell, they were returned to Poland. The Poles treated the Ukrainians as an alien element, making no distinction between Catholics and Orthodox. Only by adopting the Latin rite could Ukrainians really become Poles.

Szepticky saw the Ukrainian Catholics as a rallying-point for other Ukrainians and Russians of the Byzantine rite who might now begin to see the value of union with Rome. The Russian Empire had gone; attempts to revive the patriarchate in Moscow have led to further division and disorder, finally to the imprisonment and martyrdom of the Patriarch himself. But in order to be a rallying-point, his flock must have a strong liturgical life of their own, good monasteries, and parish clergy who would follow monastic needs. The monks of unity were originally intended to recruit help for the Ukrainians, but when the foundation was established at Amay in 1925 it inevitably attracted the Russian émigrés and their friends, who came to see and to pray. If few of them stayed, more of the monks who came to study and to use Eastern rites could not be content with the limited opportunities that Amay provided.

Difficulties were intensified through different attitudes to the Russian emigration among Catholics in general, especially in Rome. It was natural that many missionaries, accustomed to competition with Russia for influence in the East, should regard the collapse of czardom and of Orthodox power with relief. They were sorry for the Russians in exile, in a like situation to that of French émigrés after the French Revolution. They knew indeed that such exiles could be obstinate. Some of the French bishops had refused to accept the concordat between Pius VII and Napoleon and had kept up a "petite église" in schism, but not for long. "The Russian Church in exile" was only a remnant; the next generation would be Catholic, and Christians who survived persecution in the Soviet Union would welcome Catholic missionaries.

This was to ignore the Christian intelligentsia, who arrived in the West rather later, as it became more and more difficult for anyone not a dialectical materialist to hold down an academic appointment. Many of them were found in Paris where, through the Metropolitan Eulogius, they maintained their allegiance to what was left of the patriarchal administration in Moscow until 1927. They took a quite different view of the situation in Russia from "the Russian Church in exile", believing that the life of the Church persisted there and would continue in spite of communist pressures, and that the Soviet regime would not be overthrown by violence. These were the kind of Russian émigrés who made friends with Dom Lambert Beauduin and the monks of unity at Amay, who did not object to their having Anglican friends and friends in the Y.M.C.A. Matters came to a head when some of them were involved in preparations for a World Conference on Faith and Order at Lausanne in 1928.

Roman attitudes to the Ecumenical Movement at this time were coloured by the belief that it was essentially "liberal" and Modernist. This belief was shared by conservative Protestants who had all drawn out of the missionary organizations that were its seedbed, and by most Anglo-Catholics, including those who had been most successful in maintaining personal contacts with Catholics in Europe since the decision of Pope Leo XIII against the validity of Anglican orders. The Malines conversations, in which Dom Lambert was involved through a memorandum written by him for Cardinal Mercier, were originally initiated by Lord Halifax, the leader of those Anglo-Catholics whose concern for reunion was almost entirely concentrated on the problem of unity with Rome. This may give a misleading impression of Amay's Anglican contacts, which were rather with friends of the Orthodox, concerned to help them to make an adequate contribution to the World Conference at Lausanne. The encyclical *Mortalium animos*, warning Catholics

The Abbey of Maria-Laach, famous as a centre of liturgical renewal in the 1930's and the 1940's.

against involvement in the conference and in the Ecumenical Movement, made trouble for Amay which led to Dom Lambert's resignation as Prior and to his temporary departure, which lasted for some years. He did not return until the monks had moved to Chevetogne.

Maria-Laach

In 1947 in the encyclical *Mediator Dei* Pope Pius XII endorsed two of the ruling ideas of the Liturgical Movement, the participation of the whole congregation in the liturgical action, and the identity of the sacrifice of the Mass with the sacrifice of Christ himself on the cross. But he did so with warnings against exaggerations that might confuse the priestly ministries of the celebrant and of the whole people and diminish the worth of Masses without a congregation. Dom Lambert's first impression was that the warnings were more important, but he came to see in the encyclical some unexpected fulfilment for his own prophecies of change. Some of the warnings were directed against ideas circulating from Maria-Laach, a Benedictine abbey in the Rhineland, where the Abbot, Dom Ildefons Herwegen, who died in 1946, did much to impart a distinctive character to community life and liturgy. But the ideas of Maria-Laach were embodied more completely in books by Dom Odo Cassel, a younger man than Dom Lambert Beauduin, born in 1886, who died suddenly in 1948 in the course of the Easter Vigil.

The link with Solesmes and Dom Guéranger is more evident at Maria-Laach than at Amay, but the difference is also more clearly defined. Dom Herwegen regarded the Middle Ages as a time of liturgical decay, when the multiplication of low Masses introduced an element of individual, subjective devotion into what had been and ought to be objective liturgy, where the person is nothing, the Church and the community everything. In the hands of some enthusiastic disciples this antithesis could be pressed to the point of making personal devotion an imperfection. No one accused Dom Odo of doing this, but in his sensitive interpretation of the general line taken at Maria-Laach, *Das christliche Kultmysterium* (1932), translated into French as *Le mystère du culte dans le Christianisme* (1946), and into English in Britain and the United States as *The Mystery of Christian Worship* (1962), he laid himself open to criticism by reminding some who remembered the Modernist controversy of the use that Loisy had made of Protestant and secular writings on the history of religions before and after his excommunication.

Dom Odo Casel's particular contribution to the theology of the Liturgical Movement has something in common with the approach of the first two chapters of this book, which must indeed owe much to the impact of Maria-Laach on an Anglican religious community, and in particular on a pupil of Christopher Dawson. Like Loisy, Dom Casel had studied sociological and psychological explanations of early Catholicism and the mystery religions. Unlike Loisy, who was originally a lecturer on the Old Testament and had become an expert on the history of Jewish religion between the Old Testament and the New, Dom Odo had no idea of a Jesus of history other than the Jesus Christ of the New Testament, no notion of what other sort of man he could have been. But he was aware of the difficulties of treating the four gospels as historical documents. His answer to these difficulties is that Christ crucified and risen is actually present, perceived and recognized, held and known, in ourselves, our souls and bodies, in the Mass. This presence of Christ's sacrifice is a fact of experience, more certain than any historical evidence. To Loisy, so long as he remained a Catholic, the Christ of Faith and the Mother of God were the Church's symbols, part of a commitment to a myth which he shared as long as he was wanted. When the Church would not have him on these terms, they lost some of their interest, and in his later writings he multiplies reservations about the historical explanation of the genesis of Christian symbols.

Dom Casel's weakness is that he accepted uncritically explanations not of early Christianity but of the nature of the mystery religions, that were in fact largely based on the testimonies of early Christians, who regarded them as diabolic parodies of the gospel. He regarded them as part of a preparation for the gospel outside Israel, returning to views that were common, in a rather different form, among Christians after the triumph of the Church, in the fourth, fifth and sixth centuries. But by this time the pagan mysteries, with all other forms of pagan religion, had passed through a period of intense competition with Christianity. The effects of this have some parallels in India, where Hindu religion has been transformed in contact successively with Buddhism, Islam and Christianity, so that it is difficult to reconstruct as it was when the Buddha first appeared.

The real achievement of Dom Casel was to put the identity of the sacrifice of Christ on the cross and in the Mass into a form in which it would be recognized as a fact of experience, not as a scholastic theory devised to replace other theories that had overemphasized the distinction between them. He did this at a time when an increasing number of young Germans were drawn to identify themselves with the passion of Germany, in the hope that some new life might come out of it, in forms derived from the myth of the dying god, of Baldur and Odin, in songs sung in the last days of paganism, and revived in that aspect of the Nazi movement that looked back in search of a sense of identity to the natural religion of Germany, before Christianity divided Germans from their pagan past and into Protestants and Catholics. There were modified forms of this among German Lutherans, justifying anti-Semitism. But Karl Barth and the "Confessing Church" denounced them as paganism.

To some at any rate of the monks of Maria-Laach Barth was a prophetic voice who dared to speak out when Rome, for political reasons, was cautious in comment on the German situation, and had even made a concordat with Hitler and Von Papen. What Barth thought of Maria-Laach would be difficult to document. But Barthians in the Ecumenical Movement certainly saw a great difference between liturgical movements, Catholic and Anglican, and what they classified as Thomism. Soon indeed there were theologians like Canon Eugene Masure, who combined Dom Casel's insights with those of Maurice De la Taille and a number of others who had been rending in pieces what had been the accepted view of the sacrifice of the Mass at the end of the nineteenth century. Masure presented his results as in harmony with the authentic teaching of St. Thomas Aquinas, with the Council of Trent, and with the encyclical *Mediator Dei* in 1947. But this involved a new look at the position of St. Thomas in the history of theology. He no longer appeared as the founding father of scholasticism, but rather as one who was open to other influences besides Aristotle and St. Augustine, from St. John of Damascus and from the Syrian writings ascribed to Dionysius the Areopagite. As St. Thomas had survived the eclipse of scholasticism in the sixteenth century, he could and would survive another eclipse of the theology of the schools today. He was not in Barth's sense of the word a Thomist, any more than Barth himself was a Barthian.

Ecumenical Developments

Liturgical movements in the 1930s and 1940s were not limited to the Catholic Church, or in the Church of England to Anglo-Catholics. The Parish Communion movement had some Evangelical members, while many Anglo-Catholics regarded with suspicion the practice of celebrating holy communion at a service with hymns at an hour suitable for parents of young children. It was certain that they would not all be fasting. Strict Anglo-Catholics feared that this would put an end to any hope of establishing a rule for fasting communion in the Church of England. No one at this time imagined that this would soon be modified in the Roman Catholic Church.

Father A. Gabriel Hebert, of the Society of the Sacred Mission at Kelham, whose *Liturgy and Society,* published in 1935, was translated into French and had some influence on the Continent, edited in 1937 a symposium, *The Parish Communion,* on practical problems involved. A greater influence was exercised by Dom Gregory Dix, one of the Anglican Benedictines at Nashdom, through *The Shape of the Liturgy,* published in 1945. His emphasis on actions, not on texts, had some influence on Catholic developments. This needs to be seen in an Anglican context. Dom Gregory himself was one of the two first editors of *The Apostolic Tradition* ascribed to Hippolytus, but he was altogether against its use as a basis for a revised eucharistic prayer for the Church of England, especially in the invocation of the Holy Spirit, where he made the most of difficulties over the text. He found the primitive basis of eucharistic prayer not in words, but in actions, the actions of Christ at the Last Supper, when he took, blessed, broke and gave bread and wine to his apostles, telling them not to say, but to do this.

To this it could be objected that taking and blessing are not really distinct actions, and that the breaking is of the bread, not the cup, and part of the giving. But the hub of the difficulty lies in Dom Gregory Dix's insistence on the importance of the offertory as the key to differences between the eucharistic rites of East and West. "The offertory is not . . . the eucharistic oblation itself, any more than the Last Supper was itself the sacrifice of Christ. It is directed to that oblation as its pledge and starting point, just as the Last Supper looks forward to the offering on Calvary." He attached great importance to the difference between two ways of making the offertory. In one the faithful Christians bring their bread and wine, with other offerings as well, directly to the altar steps just before the great eucharistic prayer, that they may be blessed there. This is the taking, followed by blessing, breaking and giving. But in the other the offerings are brought to the sacristy earlier, or to the church door, and deposited with deacons or other ministers, that they may be prepared beforehand, as in Eastern rites and in offertory prayers out of Gallican rites that have been preserved in the Roman Mass. The earlier *Roman Ordines* contain no such prayers, but only one "secret" prayer of the celebrant as he receives the elements from representatives of the people. Contaminated as it is by Gallican infiltrations, the Roman rite still preserves the principle, that Dom Gregory Dix believed to be original, that the proper time to prepare the elements is at the offertory, not at some earlier point, as in the Dominican rite and in English and French rites of the Middle Ages.

It is fair to say that in one aspect this was a shot in a long battle between Anglo-Catholics about "Western" or "English" ceremonies. But Dom Gregory had a more serious purpose: to insist that the offertory is the liturgy of the laity, who ought to bring up the gifts themselves from the body of the church. They should then be blessed, not in offertory prayers, but in the eucharistic prayer itself. The danger of this distinction is that it may establish what it seeks to correct. By insisting on the part of the people in the action, that this is in the taking of bread and wine, before the priest blesses and breaks, and deacons give communion, he played down the people's part in the eucharistic prayer itself.

The Offertory Procession

The importance of this is quite independent of any Anglican influences, or of any impression that may have been made on Western Catholics by the Great Entrance in Eastern liturgies. The basic fact is that by all the rules every Mass requires a server or servers, who need not be ecclesiastics of any kind but can be quite ordinary laymen, and that at some Masses it has always been common to multiply these. Those therefore who desire more participation in the Mass by members of the

The offertory procession in Africa, where gifts in kind still make the best sense.

congregation, without any risk of breaking rules by introducing chants or singers or additional readings, or readers not members of the clergy, have always two obvious courses: to enlarge the choir to include, if they are daring, the voices of nuns and other women; and to multiply servers, men and boys and perhaps in some capacity girls. Various forms of offertory procession could be found in Eastern and Western rites, in the Roman *Ordines,* and in uses of the Middle Ages. It was one way of making the Mass look different, without breaking any rules, and so it happened.

After it had happened, it had to be interpreted. One way to do this was to make more of the offertory prayers, to discover their Gallican origins, and analogies to them in the rites of the East. Another, favoured by the influence of *The Shape of the Liturgy,* was to play them down and tell the congregation and the servers that what they offer is taken and transformed in the canon into the body and blood of Christ. But this offertory theology is not altogether satisfactory, where the object of the offering is concerned. The reason why rites of preparation have arisen in the East and in Gaul and Spain and have remained in the Roman liturgy is that what we offer does not simply represent the fruits of the earth and our life and work. If the sacrifice of Christ is present in the whole action of the Mass this presence cannot be limited to the time beginning after the words of consecration have been completed. There is some theological justification for treating the unconsecrated elements as symbols of Christ both in Eastern and Western rites.

The Westward Position

The rubrics of the Roman Missal as determined in 1570 allow for the possibility

163

of an altar facing the people, with the celebrant standing behind it. At the time this was very rare, in practice limited to the pope's own Mass. That prayer should be made facing the east was a tradition common to East and West. When the Roman Church came to worship in basilicas, with an apse at one end for the altar and throne and seats for the presbyters beside the bishop and behind the altar, either this was at the west end, so that the celebrant prayed across it, but the congregation turned their backs to it, or if it was at the east in the time of prayer he commonly moved to the other side of it, and prayed for the people as their representative. Only long after, in later developments of the ornaments of the altar, including the reredos, did the altar commonly come to be put right up against the east wall.

The move towards a new arrangement in the Liturgical Movement partly arose, like the offertory procession, from a desire to give the Mass a new look without contradicting any rubric. Some of the impetus came no doubt from Masses in halls and in private houses, and especially perhaps in service camps in peace and war, from Masses on board ship or in a wood for troops of scouts and girl guides, where the priest himself and his vestments must provide what ecclesiastical background there is, and difficulties in communication arising from the use of Latin can be modified by gesture and expression. It is also natural that those who wished for a greater measure of common participation in the Mass should wish to bring the altar down from remote heights and nearer the choir and the people. What is to be deplored is the insistence that celebration toward the people is proper, primitive and original. The tradition that Christians pray toward the east, in expectation of the coming of Christ, is much more clearly established than any idea that the eucharist should be celebrated around a table. The earliest pictures of Christian altars are of small, square boxes.

The Fast before Communion

The rule that holy communion ought to be the first food of the day is cited already by Hippolytus in the early third century. It had long been regarded as one that could not be dispensed except in the most extreme circumstances, generally connected with the communion of the dying, when in 1929 permission was given, but not published, authorizing "bishops and Administrators Apostolic in Russia to permit the celebration of Mass and the reception of holy communion in the afternoon or evening, on condition that a eucharistic fast of four hours from noon be observed". Like permissions were granted to military chaplains for evening Masses and evening communion from 1940 on. This has more to do with the increase in frequent, communion, commonly connected with a decree of Pope St. Pius X in 1905, than with the Liturgical Movement; but similar exhortations to frequent communion had been made by authorities previously, and had fallen on deaf ears.

The response to this in the years that followed must owe much to the same factors that favoured the growth of the Liturgical Movement, to the same desire for a closer involvement in the eucharistic life of the Church than is implied in simply hearing Mass. No doubt some of the response was made by the same people who welcomed sheets for and from a parish missal. But when the rules of fasting were relaxed, not only for soldiers, but for other kinds of workers during the war, and then in 1953 for

Concelebration; the bread is broken; the homely cups are for communion in both kinds.

those in specified circumstances who celebrated and made their communions in the evenings, communion from the reserved sacrament, outside the Mass, was still assumed to be a common form of communion for lay people. The effect of further changes, generalizing these concessions, in 1957, was to make it possible, even easy, to give general communion at Masses in the middle of the day. The further reduction of the fast to an hour in 1964 was to avoid overcrowding in Masses at the end of the morning or in the early evening.

Before the end of the pontificate of Pius XII, it had become customary for a large part of the congregation at every Mass to make their communion. The practice of confession before each communion, which had never been a rule, except for those conscious of mortal sin, but a pious custom commonly observed by devout communicants, swiftly became obsolete. Some of the needs that had promoted the rise of liturgical movements in religious houses were now the needs of every one who made their communions at a sung Mass, and wanted a form of celebration appropriate to common and corporate worship.

Concelebration

In the early Church the presbyters standing round the bishop were considered to have a share in the blessing of the eucharistic elements, and if he were ill or away, one of them would preside in his place. A similar custom persists in Eastern rites wherever priests are found together, as in monasteries. In Greece and the Middle East any priest who puts on a stole is deemed to be concelebrating, though he may

165

say nothing at all, or he may be asked by the principal celebrant to join in some of the prayers or to say some of them for the rest of the company.

In the West such concelebration had long been limited to ordinations, where the newly ordained priests follow the actions of the ordaining bishop and, saying the words after him, concelebrate with him. In Russia, and in some Eastern Churches in communion with Rome, the influence of Western theology has led to a rule that all the concelebrating priests say together the most important parts of the prayer. Some Catholic liturgists, commenting on this difference, call the Russian practice *concelebratio sacramentalis,* the Greek *concelebratio caeromonialis,* a merely "ceremonial" concelebration. But the Greeks and the other Eastern Orthodox, apart from the Russians, regard it as the original and proper form.

The desire to concelebrate more often arose in the modern Liturgical Movement first of all from the Eastern example, especially at Amay, where Dom Lambert Beauduin was aware of the problems involved, and of objections that would have to be faced. Later, especially after 1945, a growing dissatisfaction was felt about the manner of celebrating "private Masses", not so much in monasteries, where local problems could be locally met, and those who did not wish to say them too often were understood by their brethren, but above all in conferences where they had to be arranged, and priests might have to wait for an altar. Some form of concelebration was an obvious solution.

This might be managed in three ways. If every priest had his own chalice and paten, it was more like the Mass at an ordination, but really no more than a collection of low Masses said simultaneously on one large high altar instead of on a number of side-altars. If all said the words of consecration and held out their hands toward the elements in an Ukrainian or Russian manner, the Holy Office held that they might all be considered to have celebrated Mass. If, like the Greeks and Arabs, they left the speaking to a single celebrant, or shared it between them, only sharing the intention of the one who spoke the words of consecration, he had celebrated Mass, but they had not. The decision, given on May 23, 1957, was understood by some as meaning that "ceremonial" concelebration in this third manner was forbidden. However, that is a misunderstanding. It was not unlawful, but only deemed not to be a valid way of saying Mass so far as the concelebrating priests were concerned. Only the principal celebrant could fulfil any obligation by it.

All sorts of obligations arising out of stipends and foundations were here involved. These had led Pius XII in an allocution to cardinals and bishops assembled for the inauguration of a new feast of the Virgin in November 1954, to object to the idea that it is the same thing if a hundred priests concelebrate as it would be if each of them said his own Mass. Addressing an international conference on pastoral liturgy in September 1956, he said definitely that if the priests at a Mass do not each speak the words, their consecration is pure ceremony. He was evidently afraid of an assimilation of the part of the priest who concelebrates in the eucharistic sacrifice to that of the lay people who assist. He also thought that if the community Mass of priests in monastic communities was assimilated to the "ceremonial" form of concelebration, as it would be if they could celebrate in stoles from their stalls, this might very well lead to a decline in the saying of private masses, or even to an

Fr. J. Thekiso has come on a bicycle to celebrate Mass at a mission station.

extinction of the practice, on which so much devotion had been built.

The decision of the Holy Office did not forbid concelebration, but it gave the advantage to the form of it that was least popular with enthusiasts for the Liturgical Movement, and most open to practical objections, since the recitation of words in chorus by adult males is notoriously difficult to keep in time. The enthusiasts, however, were enthusiasts for obedience, and carried their zeal for it to the point of conforming with what appeared to be a direction, so that by the time of the Second Vatican Council the "Russian" way of concelebrating, rather than the primitive and Greek, had become normal in the Latin Church. Unfortunately this puts a new emphasis on the difference between concelebrating priests and others assisting at Mass. It is right that all should assist in their own order and be vested accordingly, but the distinction between ministerial priesthood and the priesthood of all Christians is clear in the whole tradition of the Western Church, and sufficiently seen in other ways.

Pius XII and Liturgical Reform

Pius XII did something to help the Liturgical Movement, not only in *Mediator Dei,* where he gave official approval, with some reserves, to most of the main ideas, but more in *Divino afflante Spiritu* (1943), when he encouraged return to older views of the inspiration of Scripture, that could be harmonized with critical inquiries into the sense of the letter, as those could not that had been devised to withstand the onslaughts of biblical criticism. But he had been elected in 1939 by those who hoped that he would stand up to Hitler and Mussolini without provoking a crisis, and throughout his pontificate he made it his business to hold a balance between conflicting tendencies. This appears in some of the measures that appeared at the time to be most controversial, such as the encyclical *Humani generis* in April 1950, which was commonly considered to be directed against those who depreciated scholasticism and entertained the idea of evolution. But it went further than any previous papal pronouncement since the controversy began, in allowing the view that the human body had evolved. The definition of the Assumption of the Virgin in the following November was so reserved that much, long commonly considered to be Catholic teaching on the subject, found no place in it. A dogma rooted not in Scripture but in liturgical song did something to strengthen the position of those who held that the Christian revelation was not entirely finished when the last apostle died, if it also built a wall against too easy a surrender to the idea that doctrine is founded on Scripture alone.

Liturgical revision in the narrower sense began with the restoration of the Easter Vigil to its ancient place on Holy Saturday night, first of all as an experiment in 1951, renewed in 1952 for three years. In 1955, when this was about to be finalized, a number of changes were made in the general rubrics of the Breviary and Missal and in the calendar, pointing to the shape of things to come, and in November of that year the Vigil was incorporated in a new liturgical order of Holy Week, including such changes as the introduction of an evening Mass on Maundy Thursday. The Mass of the pre-sanctified on Good Friday, now simply called "the solemn liturgical service", was henceforth to be celebrated in the afternoon about 3 o'clock, and in no case later than 6 p.m.

The choice of a starting-point where so much very early material remained in the liturgy is symptomatic of an increasing interest in the primitive period, when Christians were in a minority, as a norm for the future. The restored Vigil included an opportunity for all Christians to renew their baptismal vows. The Congregation of Rites observed that priests had been led to believe that "a revision of the text of the Breviary and Missal is . . . imminent". In *L'Osservatore Romano* for May 4, 1955: "Notice is hereby given that such a revision will require several years." But it was not denied that something of the kind was contemplated. The Congregation of Rites was already becoming something of a stronghold for liturgical reformers. At the Congregation of the Faith, the Holy Office, as we have seen, the direction of sympathies was in the other direction, against concelebration. Pius XII had come to recognize that the Church could not regain her ascendancy by political means, and therefore to make use of those who in the 1930s had opposed his methods of dealing with the fascist powers as Secretary of State and as Pope. But he himself by his training and experience was a political pope. He was his own secretary of state, and what concessions he made to contacts with the Ecumenical Movement were guided by a characteristic political caution.

Angelo Roncalli, elected to succeed him on October 28, 1958, was a very different kind of person. He was already seventy-six, and many supposed that a man of his age could not do much. In fact John XXIII, as he became, was pope for less than five years, but in that time made more change in the Church than any pope since Gregory VII. Dom Lambert Beauduin said to a group of his friends, including Père Louis Bouyer, immediately after the death of Pius XII, that "the cardinals, for the most part, do not know with whom they have to do. They are capable of voting for him".

The Pope and the Council

When Roncalli was sent to Bulgaria in 1925, the view of the situation commonly held at Rome was that Eastern Orthodoxy was doomed. The schism between East and West was nearly over because the Turkish and Russian Empires had both collapsed. The remnants of ancient heresies had only to be mopped up, a process that would be completed after the collapse of the U.S.S.R. As late as 1941–4 reports from parts of Russia occupied by the Germans would seem to confirm a surprising persistence of Christian faith and worship, very loosely related, if at all, to the Moscow Patriarchate. There the Metropolitan Sergius had taken advantage of the crisis to move from a discarded railway carriage to an empty embassy, where bishops were allowed to elect him Patriarch. But in Istanbul and Ankara, to a discerning eye, the matter appeared more complicated than it might appear to wishful thinking in the Roman curia. When the problems of the Church in Europe were complicated by the association of Catholic leaders with the defeated Nazis, reports from Roncalli that had been coolly received in Rome were remembered, and he was sent to deal with De Gaulle. He was critical of the Left as well as of the Right, and censures on the worker-priests in Paris, if he did not initiate them, met no opposition from him. But he had come to realize that working arrangements with communists, who make no bones about their dialectical materialism, are spiritually less dangerous than the identification of the Church with traditions in decay in such places as Spain and Hungary. In this he saw eye to eye with Barth. The story that he called him the greatest contemporary theologian is probably a legend based on his role in renewing theological debate between Catholics and Protestants, on which Pope John may well have made some jocular and provocative comment. But in fact before he was pope he knew very little directly about Protestantism. His first contacts with the French Protestant community at Taizé were made almost directly afterward, before he announced his intention to summon an ecumenical council in January 1959. Barth certainly came to see in him "a man sent from God, whose name was John", and to envisage the possibility that a Catholic theologian who had learnt from him what was really important in the insights of the Reformation might recall them to Protestants who had forgotten them.

That the role of liturgy at the Ecumenical Council was going to be important could be anticipated from the very first. Yet in spite of the fact that a new missal and breviary were supposed to be on the way, the expectations of Catholic ecumenists were rather concentrated on the powers that might be given to conferences of bishops to devise a new series of non-Roman rites, parallel to those of the East, for Churches traditionally Latin and Western in the Far East and perhaps in the Far West. What gave the matter a new turn was the favourable reception given to the material on liturgy by bishops who were otherwise very critical of material prepared for the Council in the Congregations of the Roman curia. Many of those engaged in detailed preparations were above all anxious to keep the Council on safe lines, and relied for this on the natural conservatism of most bishops. But the Congregation of Rites, unlike the Holy Office, contained an element favourable to liturgical change, and indeed committed to it. The Commission that prepared a scheme for a Constitution on Sacred Liturgy indeed had its draft modified by the Central Commission that prepared all such schemes for presentation; but even in its modified form it might expect to encounter conservative opposition.

At the second Ecumenical
Council of the Vatican, 1965.

What no one anticipated was the strength of the opposition on the floor of the Council to any prefabricated solutions, which led to a struggle over the composition of the conciliar commissions. Out of this situation emerged the decision to discuss liturgy first, a matter on which all the bishops might be expected to have ideas. Those who wanted change approved of much in the scheme for a Constitution, while conservative elements hoped that it would be rejected, and that opposition to it would be an opportunity for rallying forces in defence of other safe statements of traditional doctrine that were being unexpectedly assailed.

The unexpected happened in that some of the most conservative bishops wanted something altered. The suggestion that St. Joseph's name should be put into the canon was greeted in some quarters with ribaldry. The Pope was genuinely shocked when he heard of laughter at the expense of a devout and elderly bishop, and made the change on his own initiative. In retrospect this may seem to have been a mistake, since it closed the door to one possible option, of an unchanged Roman canon with alternatives. But no one in the opening debate had seen as far as this. Many were speaking in favour of the vernacular in the liturgy, but very few envisaged a liturgy in the vernacular all the way through, including the canon. Many, however, realized that translations of the canon were raising problems, whether or not they were liturgically used. If those who knew no Latin were to understand the Mass for the purpose of participation, they must have better translations. Probably the most serious obstacle to a conservative revision was that any clarification of the text would expose the imprecision of the original, concealed in previous translations by the transliteration of Latin words like *immaculatam hostiam,* which have acquired in other languages an hieratic sense that in Latin they do not possess.

XI Liturgical Revision

The Liturgical Constitution

The Constitution on the Sacred Liturgy of the Second Ecumenical Council of the Vatican has already in its final form, completed in December 1963, become the subject of a considerable literature. It is a mistake to think of the debate on the scheme for it primarily in terms of conflict between "integralist" traditionalists and "progressive" ecumenists. No doubt there were some, especially in Congregations of the Roman curia, who saw in liturgical change a threat to the irreformability of dogma and to the authority of the institutional Church. These were the men primarily responsible for features in the prepared documents on the sources of revelation and on the nature of the Church which the majority of the bishops in the Council would not take in the forms presented to them. The final forms of these were drastically changed. But the Constitution on the Liturgy emerged, amended indeed, but in a form nearer to what had been originally prepared by the experts on the subject than to the one, by the Central Commission, among the materials distributed to members of the Council before the sessions began. In this as in other crucial issues the diocesan bishops, supported by the Pope, prevailed over a small circle of administrators whose professional concerns led them to minimize the desirability of change in the working of the Church's machinery of administration.

But the debate on liturgy was not only or mainly between supporters and opponents of the scheme for a Constitution. When the first discussion of the scheme as a whole was complete, on November 14, only forty-six votes out of more than two thousand were given against proceeding on the general lines of it. On December 7, at the end of the first group of sessions, while 180 votes of approval were accompanied by suggestions for the amendment of the first chapter, only eleven were directly against it. The important tension, reflected in the text of the Constitution itself from first to last, was between the need for adaptations to a great variety of social and cultural circumstances, and fears that the introduction of "elements from the tradition and culture of each" of the peoples converted to the Church (article 40.1), for instance of ritual dances in Africa and Indonesia, would lead to developments which could indeed be referred to Rome, but in the nature of the case could not be fully understood there. Rejection without understanding could lead to schism, but the whole Church might suffer in reputation from rites that could be interpreted by psychoanalysts, anthropologists and Evangelical missionaries in an erotic and sinister sense.

In a speech on November 7 Bishop Van Bekkum, of Ruteng in Indonesia, spoke of the need of a place in the liturgical life of the Church for rites connected with birth, puberty, marriage, dying and death. He held that the rites of the Church themselves could only be freed from the suspicion that they were magical, if it were made plain that Christ himself is the principal minister of all the sacraments and sacramentals, built around the nucleus of his own redemptive action. This must be done in the context of a particular cultural situation. Others from Africa complained that ceremonies and traditions that did not belong to the local culture were likely to invite a magical interpretation. Africans who did not understand them could only use them in this way. Bishop O'Dwyer of Leeds, later Archbishop of Birmingham, speaking on October 30, said plainly that if every nation were allowed to make up its own order of Mass, the Roman rite would not be reformed but destroyed. Yet he would allow exceptions for African Churches, and for those in India and the Far East with cultures of their own. The Roman rite should remain a bond of unity for all the peoples of Western European culture in Europe and overseas, as the Byzantine rite is for those of Byzantine culture, although it is celebrated in different languages. The last comparison shows that he did not exclude a very wide use of translation, but the unity of the rite should remain.

The framers of the scheme had evidently intended that proposals should be made to meet pastoral needs in particular situations, and preliminary experiments made by "the competent local ecclesiastical authority" (40.1), elsewhere defined (22.1) as the bishop "as laws may determine". In article 22.2 reference is also made to "various kinds of bishops' conferences legitimately established". It was not expected that the Constitution would take its final shape until more had been done about these. Some American and Irish bishops saw no reason why they should not make their own arrangements, with proper reference to Rome, in their own dioceses, without waiting for bishops' conferences, as yet unaccustomed to make important decisions, to cut their teeth on difficult liturgical questions.

They would certainly need help from experts. This is implied in several places in the Constitution, for instance at 40.3: "Because liturgical laws are wont to involve special difficulties when applied to adaptations, particularly in the missions, men who are experts in these matters must be employed to formulate them." One way of providing help can be seen in the new provisions for the commemoration of saints, involving a much simpler classification of days, and a common of saints providing proper antiphons and prayers for "holy men and women who work for the underprivileged," plural and singular, with variations of gender. This is primarily intended as material for the making of local calendars, where memorials can be reclassified as feasts, optional memorials made obligatory, new memorials introduced, and saints assigned to their particular place in the common, which provides several Masses for instance for missionaries, some no doubt more appropriate than others in particular cases. This process was already beginning under Pius XII. In 1955 nearly all octaves were abolished and the classification of feasts greatly simplified. A completely fresh set of General Rubrics for the Breviary and Missal was put out in 1960, before the Council, on lines that were afterwards followed.

In the preface to the Constitution it is noted that "among these principles and norms there are some that can and should be applied not only to the Roman rite but to all the others". It was added, however, that "practical norms should be taken as applying only to the Roman rite". "In faithful obedience to tradition," however, the Council "declares that Holy Mother Church holds all lawfully acknowledged

174

Concelebration of the Mass at the opening of the final Session, Second Vatican Council, 1965.

rites to be of equal right and dignity". In practice this tradition had been more honoured in the breach than the observance. Very little notice was taken of the existence of Eastern rites at the Council of Trent, and at the First Council of the Vatican Eastern patriarchs in communion with Rome were made to feel uncomfortable. But at the Second Council the liturgy of the Syrian Melkites, the Milanese Mass, and the Roman rite in Old Slavonic were used in Masses during the sessions while liturgy was discussed, and the Melkite Patriarch of Antioch, Maximus IV, addressed the Council in French, since Latin was not his liturgical language, and they would not have understood Arabic. His intervention, which was pithy and to the point, was warmly applauded. The contrast in this respect with the Council of Trent is outstanding. The intention is no longer to promote uniformity, but to encourage diversity, to experiment toward a new variety of Eastern and African rites that might have analogies in parts of the West where new cultures were growing in increasing independence of the Mediterranean world. That a new liturgy with a diversity of options within it was in the outcome imposed from the centre is largely the result of concessions made, and rightly made, to those who feared that too much diversity would break up the Church.

By the terms of the Constitution the Church was committed to changes, some of them explicit as well as important. For instance, it is laid down (in 28) that "in liturgical celebrations each person, minister or layman, who has an office to perform, should do all of, but only, those parts that pertain to his office by the nature of the rite and the principles of liturgy". This principle had been applied to the special case of the Easter Vigil as early as 1951, and in the other Holy Week services in 1955. But it was now generalized. The celebrant is no longer to say everything. He is even forbidden to do it. In 31 "the revision of the liturgical books must carefully attend to rubrics for the people's parts". Reform of the mass on the lines proposed would probably have provided a number of options for alternative use at the penitential opening, and perhaps also at the offertory prayers, but left the collects, antiphons and lections for the most part to local regulation, under general provisions for a uniform relationship between saints and seasons, between ordinary Sundays and feasts to the advantage of Sundays except on the most extraordinary occasions. But it was anticipated that Latin would still be used in most of the Church. The *Kyries,* and the Latin *sanctus, benedictus qui venit* and *Agnus Dei* were and are commonly known, and many were accustomed to sing the *Gloria in excelsis* and the creed, as Catholics all over the world still sing the *Salve Regina* in Latin, while knowing and loving vernacular versions.

The pressure for more was expected to come from places remote from European culture, but in fact it seems to have come from the centre, through anxiety lest experiments on the periphery should get out of hand unless more material was provided for their use by those who understood the issues. This was already plain on the issue of concelebration, where the scheme was amended from the floor to make it more like the draft originally prepared by liturgical experts, and cut down by the Central Commission for preparing documents. The final result gives wider opportunities in more explicit terms, but also provides for more precise regulation, in terms not easy to reconcile with the promise of a wider diversity in rite.

The matter had been discussed a great deal in many places before and after the comments of Pius XII on the subject in 1954 and 1956, and the ruling of the Holy Office in 1957. These as we have seen were unfavourable to the practice, but in 1962–3 the tide was running the other way. In an article of the Constitution (57) it is laid down that "both in the East and in the West concelebration . . . has remained in use". This was to make the most of the rites used in the ordination of priests, where they concelebrate with the bishop. Concelebration is called a rite "whereby the unity of the priesthood is manifested. Permission for its use is extended to the evening Mass on Maundy Thursday", as well as the Mass earlier in the day for the consecration of the chrism, where it had been allowed and common since 1955, to Masses "during Councils, bishops' conferences and synods", and "at the Mass for the blessing of an abbot". Other uses are made to depend on "the permission of the Ordinary", generally meaning the bishop, "at conventual Mass, and at the principal Mass in churches where the needs of the faithful do not require that all the priests available should celebrate individually", and also at other kinds of meetings of priests. "It is for the bishop however to regulate the discipline of concelebration in his diocese." The right of priests to celebrate their own Mass is carefully safeguarded, with limitations. "A new rite for concelebration is to be inserted into the Pontifical and the Roman Missal." It was inevitable that this should follow the ruling of 1957, so far as the meaning of the term is concerned, that it means a Mass where all priests concelebrating say the words of consecration. But in the outcome the new rubrics say, at 170: "The parts pronounced by all the concelebrants together should be so said in recitation that they say them in a low voice and the voice of the principal celebrant is clearly heard.

This is the point at which the Constitution comes closest to regulating detail, and it has probably been critical for the future of the missal. It made it necessary to begin with a further revision of the General Rubrics of 1960, to provide the conditions necessary for concelebration, a free-standing altar, "so that ministers can easily walk around it and Mass can be celebrated facing the people". This may be fixed or movable. Mass "in other places where the eucharist is not regularly celebrated" is now regarded as normal. Concelebration facing the people in a manner which the Eastern Orthodox regard as peculiarly Russian has certainly eased some problems, such as the provision of altars for private Masses, and some of the problems arising from these, but created others, not all of them foreseen, such as a kind of architectural iconoclasm in the treatment of the reredos and the high altar, when that has been designed in a manner characteristic of the West from the thirteenth to the twentieth century. It probably made it more difficult to postpone the problem of the Roman canon.

Some evidently expected that the use of the Roman rite would come to be limited to lands under the direct influence of European culture, as rites developed in India and the Far East, and probably in parts of Africa, in something like the relation to the Roman rite as those of some Eastern Churches in communion with Rome, whose rites have come to contain a Latinized element. This would no doubt have given rise to a host of further problems, but the Roman canon might still have been used in Latin, or in a limited number of approved translations, where the Roman rite remained, without too many immediate difficulties. The real difficulty was and is, that the translations found in devotional books, coloured by the piety of the nineteenth century, are not only unsuitable for liturgical speech, for which they were never designed, but often an obstacle to real understanding of words and their meanings. If the Roman rite was now going to be celebrated in a new way, with fuller participation by the whole congregation, everywhere from China to Peru, the nettle must be grasped.

The Problem of the Canon

As we have seen, at the beginning of this century liturgists were divided in their estimate of the Roman canon. For Father Adrian Fortescue and others, Catholic as well as Anglican, the text was "dislocated", hallowed by long use, but in its present form incapable of being understood. For Edmund Bishop and a few of his friends, it was understood in the light of its immediate historical background, as a primitive text that took something like its present shape before the definition of the Trinity and the Incarnation was yet complete, and long before specific questions of eucharistic theology were raised in the West. This interpretation of the canon was congenial to some Anglicans who wanted a liturgy with the minimum of doctrinal definition, and not altogether unacceptable to others, who generally agreed with Adrian Fortescue, but hoped that a eucharistic prayer containing an explicit invocation of the Holy Spirit might be regarded by Roman Catholics as superior to their own. In 1927 and 1928 this line in Anglican liturgical revision suffered defeat in proposals for an alternative Prayer Book in England, but it persisted in places like South Africa, and it came back again in the liturgy of the United Church of South

India (1948–50), where, under the influence of the rites of Kerala, used by Catholics of the Syro–Malabar and Syro–Malankara communities, and by the Syrian Jacobites, acclamations by the people were added: "Thy death, O Lord, we commemorate, thy resurrection we confess, and thy second coming we await. Glory be to thee, O Christ." A little later the people say: "We give thanks to thee, we praise thee, we glorify thee, O Lord our God." These follow the narrative of the institution of the eucharist, but precede the invocation: "And we most humbly beseech thee, O merciful Father, to sanctify with thy Holy Spirit, us and these thine own gifts of bread and wine, that the bread which we break may be the communion of the body of Christ, and the cup which we bless the communion of the blood of Christ. Grant that being joined together in him, we may all attain to the unity of the faith, and may grow up in all things unto him who is the Head, even Christ, our Lord. . . . "

The scheme for reunion in South India had been opposed by Anglo-Catholics in sympathy with Western traditions, and so the United Church had escaped the pervasive influence of Dom Gregory Dix and his *Shape of the Liturgy* (1945), but the South India rite attracted favourable comment from Catholic liturgists, some of whom had been consulted while it was in process of formation. The same line was followed in a draft *Liturgy for Africa* (1964), which became the basis for *A United Liturgy for East Africa* (1966), intended to be used by Anglicans, Lutherans, Moravians, Methodists and others involved in a scheme of reunion in Kenya and Tanganyika on lines somewhat similar to those developed in India and Ceylon. Here the acclamations have changed direction, and are: "His death, O Father, we proclaim: his resurrection we confess: his coming we await. Glory be to thee, O Lord." The invocation of the Spirit is nearer to the *Apostolic Tradition* of Hippolytus: "Accept us in him, we beseech thee, that we may be filled with thy Holy Spirit, and made one in thy Church which thou art gathering together from all the ends of the earth." In the *Liturgy for Africa*, composed by the Anglican Archbishop of Uganda, the final reference to the *Didache*, "gathering together from all the ends of the earth", was not there, but "thy holy Church" is further defined as "the body of thy Son, Jesus Christ our Lord".

In the 1960s Anglicans and Catholics had a common problem in devising materials that might be used in lands where liturgical scholarship was not easily available on the spot. Both were aware of objections to anything that might minimize the central significance of the narrative of the institution in Western tradition, Catholic, Anglican and Protestant, strongest of all in Lutheranism, where the tradition is to have nothing else in the prayer of consecration. Catholics and some Anglicans were drawn to see fresh significance in the ancient liturgy of Alexandria, where the invocation of the Holy Spirit precedes and follows the narrative of the institution, and to look for examples of this in Western as well as in African prayers, not only in the first Anglican *Prayer Book* of 1549, but in some Mozarabic Masses, for instance in the Missal of Ximenez for the third Sunday after Pentecost, where the first invocation is clearly consecratory.

It is on these lines that the second, third and fourth prayers of new Roman rite took shape, using materials from Hippolytus, from Eastern liturgies, and from the

Scene of first communion in France.

non-Roman rites of the West, Gallican and Mozarabic. But they would not have been made at all if the revision of the Roman canon had proved possible. Essays in this direction were made by Hans Küng, among others. But they were chiefly concerned with removing the intercessions to another place, and simplifying or reducing the commemoration of saints, so as to make the text run more smoothly. It was found impossible to supply what is lacking without in effect writing a new canon. To remedy what is not there because the question had not arisen at the time when the canon was written is inevitably to suggest that the theology of the framers was in some way defective. The canon was made by the fathers and saints of the Roman Church, who were truly inspired to meet the needs of their day. It cannot be reformed, and it ought to be treasured, but it needs to be supplemented, like the creeds and the Scriptures.

The New Missal

In considering developments since the conclusion of the Second Vatican Council, it seems better to review them in the form in which they stand in the new Roman Missal of 1970. No doubt much will be written on the process of liturgical change, both in Latin and in translation, which always involves some change in adaptation to the forms of a different language, but the material for this is simply not available, not because of any deliberate policy of secrecy, but because so much is still laid up in the memories of those concerned, and cannot be constructed out of drafts and versions, where they still exist.

It seems best to begin with the Ordinary in the strict sense, including the penitential opening, the provision for intercessions, and the offertory prayers before we proceed to the eucharistic prayers one by one. Penitential rites in a variety of

179

forms appear in the missals printed on the eve of the Reformation. They were standardized in the Tridentine *Missale Romanum,* but not regarded as a proper part of the rite itself. The introit did not begin until the preparation was complete and, at solemn Masses, the altar censed. The *Kyries* were then to be said or sung by the celebrant and servers alternatively. In the new missal, at Masses with a congregation, the introit is to be sung as the ministers enter, but it is still in the old place when Mass is said simply by the priest and his server. At such Masses they prepare themselves by mutual confession and absolution, without a psalm. The confession is made only "to God and to you, my brother," although the prayers of the Virgin and all the saints are invoked. At Masses with a congregation they may be involved in this, or simply called upon to repent of their sins in silence. Among other forms of penitential preparation there is one that is based on the traditional rite of *Asperges,* where holy water is blessed, sometimes with the addition of salt, and sprinkled on the congregation. Where the *Kyries* are included, as they are in this and several of the other rites, they are not repeated.

The *Gloria in excelsis* follows on all Sundays and feasts, and the collect proper to the Mass. There are two or three lessons, with a responsorial psalm between them, including a respond to be recited by the whole congregation. The sermon follows on Sundays and holy days of obligation, and the Nicene Creed on Sundays and solemnities, feasts of the highest rank, less often than in the past. For the general intercession after this the Latin provides a number of models. These are translated into English, but in fact a greater variety of forms are used in ways that will encourage ministries of intercession in members of the congregation. At this point free prayer can develop, where the influence of charismatic movements is felt.

So far, the maximum of flexibility has been found. The position at the offertory is less happy. A procession is desired, but not prescribed. The offertory prayers in the Tridentine Missal at this point are all infiltrations from other texts into the Roman Mass in the Middle Ages. All were originally written to bless the elements at some earlier point, before the offertory, that they might be introduced into the rite as symbols in terms anticipating their future use. All that remains of this in the new missal is an abbreviated version of the celebrant's prayer at the mixing of water and wine, that "through the mystery of this water and wine we may be made sharers in the divinity of him who condescended to be a partaker of our humanity"; his prayer as he washes his hands, one other prayer *In spiritu humilitatis,* all spoken quietly, and the versicle and respond, *Orate fratres, ut meum ac vestrum sacrificium acceptabile fiat apud Deum Patrem omnipotentem.* This also is medieval, with the response, which the Tridentine Missal puts in the mouths of the *circumstantes,* "of those present," and not of the server alone. This was one of the few places where some response from the people was expected in the Middle Ages.

Those who prepared the missal originally intended to leave this, and the "collect over the oblation," proper to every Mass, that immediately follows, before "Lift up your hearts," but no other offertory prayers. This was resented as playing down the offertory altogether, and a new set of prayers was introduced to be said by the priest as he receives the paten with the bread and the chalice filled with wine. These are said quietly if the offertory antiphon or some other chant is being sung, but if not he is allowed to speak them so that the people may reply. Each time he receives one of the elements he says "Blessed are you, Lord, God of all creation. Through your goodness we have . . . to offer" this bread "which earth has given and human hands have made. It will become for us the bread of life". He continues afterward to say that "this wine . . . fruit of the vine and work of human hands . . . will become our spiritual drink". The people reply to either, "Blessed be God for ever."

The Latin says of both *quem tibi offerimus,* which is not exactly translated into English. The translators at this point may have had sympathy with the motives that led the authors of the original draft to want to do without prescribed prayers at the offertory of the elements. If they had done so, no doubt many priests would have used the old ones, but some might also have thought that the bread and wine "which we have to offer" are more properly offered in the eucharistic prayer. It is true that they do represent, among other created things, the fruits of the earth and of human toil, but what makes them a sacrifice is that they are taken up and transubstantiated in the sacrifice of Christ. There are not two sacrifices, a sacrifice of bread and wine in the offertory and another of the body and blood of Christ made present in and after the consecration, but one, representing ourselves, our souls and bodies, taken up into the sacrifice of Christ.

The Eucharistic Prayers

The first is rightly called the Roman canon. The words are nearly the same, and many of the rubrics for gestures are still there, if some of these have been changed, and more simplified. Some of the saints in the *Communicantes* are in brackets, as is *Per eumdem Christum Dominum nostrum. Amen,* at the end of this prayer. This can be left out, and the saints from James and John to Cosmas and Damian, but St. Joseph is in, inserted by Pope John on his own initiative. Of the other changes in the words some are in brackets, like the names of the saints in the *Nobis quoque peccatoribus* from St. Ignatius of Antioch to the rather mysterious Anastasia, and can be omitted like the endings of the *Hanc igitur oblationem,* the *supplices te rogamus,* and the *Memento* of the dead. The important change is in the actual narrative of the institution, where the words, *mysterium fidei,* between "This is the chalice of my blood; of the new and eternal testament" and "which is poured out for you and for many", are not omitted but postponed until after HOC FACITE IN MEAM COMMEMORATIONEM. This in capitals replaces *Haec quotiescumque feceritis, in mei memoriam facietis,* which were always in small type. *Mysterium fidei* in its new place is a clue for the acclamations of the congregation: *Mortem tuam annuntiamus, Domine, et tuam resurrectionem confitemur, donec venias,* or in other forms.

The changes in the rubrics are slight, but include some that must be intended to reduce or remove the discrepancy between the words and actions of the Roman canon and the accepted theology of eucharistic consecration that was a subject of complaint from Peter of Blois at the time of Pope Innocent III and again at the Council of Trent. The utmost care has been taken to respect the traditions of Western Christendom in the matter of the moment of consecration, even at the expense of rituals that reflect older beliefs more congenial to most of those who work for liturgical change.

The objections of traditionalists who distinguish between the first eucharistic prayer and the Roman canon are really to the translations rather than to the Latin text. But some of these should please them. *Haec* in the *supplices te rogamus* is not simply "these things" but "this sacrifice" to be taken by "your angel" to "your altar in heaven". No attempt is made to translate *sanctum sacrificium, immaculatam hostiam*, as spoken of Melchisedech's sacrifice of bread and wine, meaning originally no doubt no more than "a holy and spotless sacrifice", but commonly understood in terms that require a reference to the body and blood of Christ. At other points the translation may be more open to question. *Panem sanctum vitae aeternae* becomes simply "the bread of life", and *Haec munera, haec sancta sacrificia illibata* "these gifts we offer you in sacrifice". *Placatus* is not translated in the *Hanc igitur oblationem*, except by "Father, accept this offering." "Be pleased to accept" would actually be enough, but might be taken to translate the idea of propitiation controversially, although in the ancient language of sacrifice "be propitious" meant no more than "give signs of favour" in the auspices, and so it was probably understood in Rome in the fourth and fifth centuries. There may be other objections, but the absence of any equivalent for *illibata*, which may be the most serious, is very intelligible in view of the difficulty of understanding quite what it means. "Ordained", "appointed", "perfected" are all possible, but nothing is yet complete.

The three new prayers, as is to be expected, have some common features, and it may be best to deal with these first, before considering their distinctive characteristics. All invoke the blessing of the Holy Spirit on the oblation before the narrative of the institution, and on the communicants after the commemoration of the work of Christ that follows this. They then proceed with prayer for the Church, including the commemoration of saints.

In the second prayer the first invocation of the Spirit has a form that is found in Gallican prayers: *Haec ergo dona, quaesumus, Spiritus tui rore sanctifica* [with the dew of your Spirit] *ut nobis Corpus et + Sanguis fiant Domini nostri Iesu Christi*. The *nobis* is from the *Quam oblationem* in the Roman canon, where "for us" had been taken as meaning for our communion only, not only by the Reformers but by some precursors of theirs in the Middle Ages. In the third prayer it comes in a context derived from a Mozarabic Mass, and prays "that these gifts which we have brought you to be hallowed, you would sanctify by your Spirit (*quae tibi sacranda detulimus, eodem Spiritu sanctificare digneris*) *ut Corpus et + Sanguis fiant . . .*" without *nobis*. And so in the fourth prayer: "*Quaesumus igitur, Domine, ut idem Spiritus Sanctus haec munera sanctificare dignetur, ut Corpus et + Sanguis fiant Domini nostri Iesu Christi*."

The narrative of the institution follows in different forms. The form in the Roman canon had to be amended to bring *Mysterium fidei* to the end for the acclamations. To amend it further to make a common form for all the prayers would have aroused resentment, but the differences between them are not sufficient to require comment. What follows is much more important. In the second prayer, based on Hippolytus, and originally proper to the ordination of the bishop, it is rather slight: "Mindful therefore of his death and resurrection, we offer you, Lord, the bread of life and the chalice of salvation" (more than in the original prayer of Hippolytus, which has simply "this bread and cup"), "giving you thanks that you

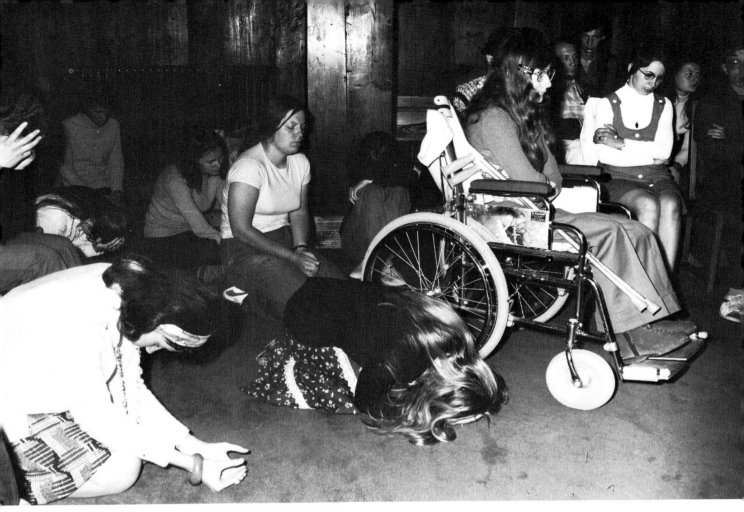

have counted us worthy to stand before you and minister to you". The form in the third prayer is much stronger. Here we remember not only the death and resurrection, but the ascension: "Ready to greet him when he comes again, we offer you in thanksgiving this holy and living sacrifice." In the fourth prayer, where we also remember Christ's "descent among the dead [*ad inferos*]" and expect his coming in glory, "*offerimus tibi eius Corpus et Sanguinem, sacrificium tibi acceptabilem et toti mundo salutare* [for the salvation of the whole world]".

Père Louis Bouyer, with reference to the third prayer in an essay in *The New Liturgy*, edited by Lancelot Sheppard (1970), says that this "most traditional expression of the eucharistic sacrifice removes from it every appearance even of a sacrifice that we offer and consecrate ourselves". It cannot be "anything else than the sacrament that Christ left for us to be united in his one and perfect offering". He relates this "central expression" of the sacrifice in the third prayer to the researches of Joachim Jeremias, a distinguished Protestant commentator into the meaning of "in memorial of me" in successive editions of his *Eucharistic Words of Jesus*. If Père Bouyer is right, this points to a breakthrough, not only in the less important differences between East and West over the moment of consecration in the eucharist, but in the crisis in the sixteenth century over the meaning of sacrifice. This

The handicapped and those who live under strain pray for help and healing.

was certainly connected with a common understanding at that time of expressions in the *unde et memores* of the sacrifice of Christ made present on the altar in the words of institution and elevated on the altar just before, that now he was sacrificed again. Not all the schoolmen thought of the sacrifice of the Mass as consequent upon the consecration, but some, following Duns Scotus rather than St. Thomas, certainly did so. The first prayer, perhaps the second, just conceivably the fourth, could be read in this **way**. But if the first and second are henceforth to be understood in the clearer terms of the third and fourth together, this misunderstanding is eliminated. Consecration is sacrifice and sacrifice consecration.

The second invocation of the Spirit is not quite so important. In the second prayer, following the text of Hippolytus, we pray "*ut Corporis et Sanguinis Christi participes a Spiritu Sancto congregemur in unum*". In the third, which contains another element in the original prayer of Hippolytus, we are to be "filled with the Holy Spirit, and found to be one body, one spirit in Christ". In the fourth, where the Latin is very expressive, we "*qui ex hoc uno pane participabunt et calice . . . in unum corpus a Sancto Spiritu congregati, in Christo hostia viva perficiantur, ad laudem gloriae tuae.* The English translations do not do justice to this. In the common version "And by your Holy Spirit, gather all who share this bread and wine, into the one body of Christ, a living sacrifice of praise", objection has been taken to "this bread and wine" as a translation of "*hoc uno pane . . . et calice*". But we need also a better translation of what follows – "that we may be made in Christ a living sacrifice, to the praise of your name".

The prayers for the Church that follow are not part of the original text of the prayer of Hippolytus, but they naturally follow from his prayer that we may be gathered into one, and they have certainly been in the Roman canon since very near the beginning of its history. They are not developed at length as in the Eastern liturgies, even in the fourth prayer, which is nearest to these, and some would have wished to omit them altogether, as duplicating the general intercession at the end of the liturgy of the Word, before the offertory, where prayers of this kind are also found in Eastern liturgies; and the "names", the intercessions for persons and causes are in the Gallican and Mozarabic rites, as perhaps they were once in Rome. But prayers for the dead, which have a special place in them, are found in this place in the prayers of Serapion, as well as in the developed liturgy of the Church of Alexandria. In view of the general preoccupation of the Egyptians with the dead, with the care of tombs and of bodies, it is not altogether unlikely that they spread from there into other places, at any rate in this special position. The commemoration of saints is naturally associated with them, and this could not easily be moved from the canon to another place in the liturgy. In the third prayer it stands before all prayer for the living, in the second and fourth in association with the doxology at the end. It does not seem to be necessary to say more about this.

The complaint of theological imprecision in these prayers may apply with some justice to the second, based on a primitive text. It might have been better to make the greater part of the prayer of Hippolytus, before the narrative of the institution, into a prayer after the *sanctus,* rather than a preface. The second prayer would then have been used with other prefaces like the first and the third prayer, but it would

Singing in the sanctuary. The guitar can be a channel of inspiration.

not have been so short, and there are occasions when a short prayer is needed. The third and the fourth prayers are alternative models, pointing in rather different directions. The theological wealth of the fourth prayer is great, and it could be the subject of a chapter by itself, but much of its background lies in material not covered in the earlier chapters of this book—in the great liturgies of the East, especially in various versions of the *Anaphora of St. Basil.* Père Joseph Gelineau, in another essay in the same book on *The New Liturgy,* from which Père Bouyer's contribution has been cited, notes that "this prayer can hardly be preceded by the Creed without danger of burdensome repetition". It is in truth a confession of faith in prayer and praise, and many will recognize this as a merit. However, it should be noticed that of the Eastern Churches with *anaphoras* of this kind, only the Armenians have kept just one of them, and they have several no longer in use. The Byzantines were reduced to two, which are really variations on one, by some of the same circumstances that drove Rome to a like solution. The Syrian Jacobites have eighty somewhere in their books, and the Ethiopians fourteen, each a distinct composition, some of them eccentric and rather odd. There may be parts of the world where such an approach to the problem of liturgical composition will find favour, but the third prayer which allows the use of proper prefaces seems a more probable model for Europe and America.

In this the *post-sanctus* begins with a reminiscence of the Mozarabic Mass for the Feast of the Circumcision: *"Vere incomparabiliter te esse sanctum, Domine, omnis profitetur a te condita creatura, a quo et creantur et sanctificantur omnia."* In a new prayer this runs: *"Vere sanctus es, Domine, et merito te laudat omnia a te condita creatura,* [Father, you are holy indeed, and all creation rightly gives you praise]." The English translation, here adequate and accurate, continues: "All life, all holiness comes from you through your Son, Jesus Christ our Lord, by the working of the Holy Spirit." There follows a reminiscence of the *Didache:* "From age to age you gather a people to yourself, so that from east to west a perfect offering may be made to the glory of your name." The Latin of "perfect offering" is *oblatio munda,* the "pure offering" of Malachi 1:11, which the Christian Fathers, from St. Justin Martyr onward, identified as the eucharist.

The invocation of the Spirit, already considered, follows, and leads to the narrative of the institution, beginning in the Mozarabic manner followed in Anglican prayer books, "On the same night in which he was betrayed. . . ." The memorial of Christ's saving work in its full magnificence, "the central expression of the eucharistic sacrifice", as has already been said, is linked with the second invocation of the Holy Spirit by a like link in the *post-mysterium* of the Wednesday after Easter in the Missal of Ximenez: *"Cognosce precamur omnipotens Deus victimam: qua intercedente placatus es."* In the new Latin form *agnoscens Hostiam, cuius voluisti immolatione placari* is translated into English as "and see the victim whose death has reconciled us to yourself," not "yourself to us". This translation is not satisfactory, either verbally or as theology. We may not eliminate from our theological thinking the mysterious working of the will of God to be moved by the death of Christ, however undesirable we may think some explications and developments of this theme have been. The second invocation leading out of this has already been considered. The result is a *post-mysterium,* as well as a *post-sanctus,* as satisfying as anything in the Mozarabic and Gallican missals, and much more coherent than the corresponding prayers of the Roman canon.

Père Bouyer notes resemblances between Mozarabic prayers and those of the Syrian Jacobites. He thinks them "importations from the Syrian liturgy at a period of transition while it still retained the flexibility that it was to lose in the east after the end of the fourth century". They are not "more or less late additions" as some liturgists have thought. But among the Jacobites flexibility lasted into the Middle Ages. No doubt at Rome and Constantinople they were considered Monophysite heretics, but this did not prevent the Syrian merchants who found their way into China and India from reaching Spain, and there entering into communion with the local churches. Where merchants go, wandering monks often follow, who may exercise influence on liturgy.

The third prayer is made to accompany prefaces. The number of these in the new rite is truly astonishing. Most of them are for particular occasions and themes. More might have been done to develop the theme of creation, whose proper place is before the *sanctus,* on lines that again are found in Gallican and Mozarabic as well as in Eastern liturgies. But these would need to be adapted to modern understandings of the cosmic process. If there come to be more prefaces, as there probably will, there seems no reason why these should not be accompanied by more prayers *post-sanctus* and *post-mysterium.* Freedom in this indeed had some odd consequences in the West in the early Middle Ages, especially in Masses of the saints, but such prayers would now be controlled by the need to make two invocations, on the elements before and on the communicants after the central climax in the narrative of the institution and the commemoration of the work of Christ, which might well become constant in something like the form found in the third prayer. So we might secure something of unity and coherence of the great Eastern anaphoras, without departing from the Western tradition of uniformity at some fixed central points. Perhaps it would have been in better accordance with this tradition if the acclamations had been fixed. We may find in time whether more is needed than "Christ has died, Christ is risen, Christ will come again". This has the advantage of keeping the tradition that all eucharistic prayer is addressed to the Father, though the Eastern rites from which the acclamations are derived also address the Son, as in "Dying you destroyed our death, rising you restored our life. Lord Jesus, come in glory", and in the simple Irish invocation, redolent of adoration after the elevations, "My Lord and my God".

Masses Proper to Occasions

It is impossible in the space available to do justice to the wealth of material in the proper parts of the new missal. The common of saints is intended to be adapted for use in local calendars. The reduction in the general calendar is intended to promote variety in these by making many memorials optional, that have less universal interest, as well as to eliminate some whose legends give rise to problems. But St. George, who is one of these, is not only retained but provided with a magnificent collect: *Magnificantes, Domine, potentiam tuam, supplices exoramus, ut, sicut sanctus Georgius dominicae fuit passionis imitator, ita sit fragilitatis nostrae promptus adiutor.* Among saints recently canonized, the martyrs of Uganda have a collect derived from an unlikely source, one of the "Neo-Gallican" missals of the eighteenth century, but it contains an expression of Tertullian, "the blood of the martyrs is the seed of Christians", and so an echo of the first persecutions.

A number of Masses have been provided for special needs in prayer for the Church and the world, for the unity of Christians, and for peace and justice. A new set of "ritual Masses" restore special formulas for the stages of Christian initiation, like those of the ancient "scrutinies" of the catechumens during Lent, for a married couple, not only at the wedding, but also on wedding days, and for other anniversaries, for various forms of profession to the religious life, and of ordination

Praying together in a large charismatic group in Rome.

to ministries in the Church, not only to "holy orders" in the technical sense. The Masses for the dead have been enlarged by provision for every kind of particular situation from the death of a pope to the death of a child who has not been baptized. They have also been transformed by a new stress on the share of Christians in Christ's resurrection, which is also found in the prayers for the dead in the three new eucharistic prayers. Each of these contains clauses to be used specially at requiem Masses.

Not all of this material is of equal literary merit or theological value, but considering the short time that has elapsed since the moment when liturgical revision became a practical possibility, in 1951–5 where the propers of particular Masses were concerned, and in 1962–3 for the order of the Mass, the achievement can be described as miraculous in the sense that it is impossible, at least as yet, to perceive any social, cultural or psychological factors sufficient to explain it. Even the Latin style of the collects, in the cultural conditions of the twentieth century, defies every canon of probability. Those who write off the revision as deterioration can find arguments to help them in the style of some of the translations, still more in the ways in which the new liturgy is commonly rendered by those who do not enter into the spirit and intentions of those concerned in its framing, or share their sense of tradition.

It is impossible not to respect the integrity of the Russian Old Believers, the Greek Old Calendarists, and the "Russian Church in exile". The same respect must be given to Roman Catholic "Traditionalists". But all such groups, including conservative Protestants, and those who cling most tenaciously to the hope of recovering the original gospel of Christ by approved methods of historical research, are in danger of confounding the worship of God with the idolatry of their culture. Such perils may also await zealots for the new liturgy, but at present they know that we have not come to the end of the story.

The Bible, the Church and the Mass

The development of biblical studies among Catholics in the last forty years is probably better understood by conservative Protestants, who see it as moving away from them, than by liberals in the theological schools, who think it is moving toward them. They are naturally struck by resemblances between Catholic approaches and those of Anglo-Catholics as they began to come to terms with biblical criticism at the end of the nineteenth century. But there is really a closer analogy with an earlier group of Anglicans, disciples of S. T. Coleridge and friends of F. D. Maurice, who interested themselves in the approach of the Greek Fathers to the spiritual interpretation of Scripture at a time when others engaged in critical controversy were simply interested in asking "Is the Bible true?"

The spiritual interpretation of the Scriptures has never died out. It will always persist so long as meditations are made on a text and sermons preached. But it suffered in reputation when Anglican scholars from Westcott to Sir Edwyn Hoskyns, the translator of Barth's commentary on the Epistle to the Romans, were accused of evading the issues by taking the Gospel of St. John seriously, without committing themselves clearly on its value as a record of events. It began to be taken

Archbishop Marcel Lefèbvre gives communion after celebrating a Tridentine Mass in London.

more seriously again in contacts between Eastern Orthodox and Western Christians, Catholic, Anglican and Protestant, in the years between the two world wars, as biblical scholars began to understand the New Testament as a series of testimonies made in Christian worship. This was developed by German Protestants into what is called "form criticism", and used by them chiefly to identify causes for the development of "early Catholicism". That spiritual or mystical interpretation depends on an oracular view of inspiration still appears to be a fundamental presupposition in the English theological schools.

In the 1960s this came to be assailed from a new direction, through the penetration of pentecostal movements into the main-line Protestant denominations, first of all in America, with ideas of prophetic inspiration which some conservative Protestants regarded as undermining the fundamental difference between Scripture and other inspired literature, while liberals were worried by the reappearance of questions concerning the discernment of spirits, and demons and demonic influences. As Catholic scholars became involved in such movements, first in the American and then in the Roman universities in the aftermath of the Second Vatican Council, a new relationship began to develop between conservative Protestants, who had always been aware that they had something in common with Catholics in resistance to the negative conclusions of biblical criticism, and Catholic biblical scholarship, supposed by liberal Protestants to be slowly moving, as Anglo-Catholic scholarship had moved, in the liberal direction.

As the Scriptures come to be read and understood by the whole congregation in the context of the Mass, their original role in Christian tradition begins to be rediscovered. The sources of Christian doctrine are not the Bible alone, as

More ceremonial movement
during the Mass for the carnival
at Notting Hill.

Opposite: Freedom in prayer in
the context of the Mass.

Protestants have said, or the Bible and other apostolic tradition, as Catholics used to say, but the Bible in the tradition of the Church which is still engaged in receiving the Scriptures. It may well be that three lessons on every Sunday is not the best way of providing material for preaching, or for meditation, and that the lectionary in the new missal is otherwise open to criticism, but at any rate it does help to put the Bible into a proper context, not only for Catholics.

In the early Church hearers and catechumens came to the readings in the first part of the synaxis, and left before the prayers of the faithful. Now an increasing number of interested observers are drawn into full participation in the liturgy, some to the point of making their communions, and these will not always be baptized Christians of another confession. The problem of prayer with those who come to pray with Catholic Christians, not only in the Mass, but elsewhere, is probably more important, and certainly more urgent, than schemes for reunion with ecclesial bodies of baptized Christians outside the institutional structures of the Church. The schism between East and West is a division within those structures, which happened gradually and will be healed slowly. That is the reason why Catholics can be happy to receive communion from Orthodox behind the iron curtain and to admit Orthodox of the Dispersion to their altars. The same is true of other Eastern Churches on the way to heal schisms that have arisen largely out of their isolation. But it is impossible to be indifferent to the serious causes of the alienation of baptized Christians in the West from the structures of the Western Church. They need to be healed, and they are being healed, but barriers are not removed by gate-crashing.

Select Bibliography

Collections of Texts

Ancient Liturgies of the Gallican Church (ALGC), ed. J. M. Neale and G. H. Forbes, Burntisland, Scotland, 1855.

Concilium Tridentinum, ed. S. Ehses *et al.*, Fribourg in Breisgau, Switzerland, 1904–38.

Commentary on the Documents of Vatican II, ed. Herbert Vorgrimler, London and New York, 1967–9.

Epistolae Romanorum Pontificum, ed. A. Thiel, Braunsberg, Germany, 1868.

Henry Bradshaw Society's publications (HBS).

Liturgy in English, ed. Bernard Wigan, London, 2nd ed. 1964.

Modern Anglican Liturgies, 1958–68, ed. Colin Buchanan, London, 1968.

Ordines Romani, ed. Michel Andrieu, Louvain, 1931–51.

Patrologia Graeco-Latina, ed. J. P. Migne, Paris, 1857–66.

Patrologia Latina (PL), ed. J. P. Migne, Paris, 1844–55.

Sacrosanctum Oecumenicum Concilium Vaticanum II; Constitutiones, Decreta, Declarationes, Rome, 1966.

"Apostolic Church Order" in Adolf Harnack, *Sources of the Apostolic Canons*, E.T., London, 1895, or G. Horner, *Statutes of the Apostles*, Cambridge, 1904.

Burkhard (or Burchard), Joannes. "Ordo Missae" in *Tracts on the Mass*, HBS, 1904.

Hippolytus, *Apostolic Tradition*, ed. Gregory Dix, London and New York, 1937. This is based on R. H. Connolly, The *So-called Egyptian Church Order and Derived Documents*, Cambridge, 1916. Dix's edition was revised by Henry Chadwick, London (not New York), 1968. A better edition is *La tradition apostolique*, by Dom Bernard Botte, Münster, Germany, 1963 and 1972.

Leonine Sacramentary, ed. C. Feltoe, Cambridge, 1896; and again as *Sacramentarium Veronense*, by L. C. Mohlberg *et al.*, Rome, 1956.

Liber Mozarabicus Sacramentorum, ed. Dom Marius Ferotin, Paris, 1912.

Liber Ordinum, ed. Dom Marius Ferotin, Paris, 1904.

Vatican Council II; The Conciliar and Post-Conciliar Documents, ed. Austin Flannery, O.P., 1975, Long Island, New York, and Dublin.

Liber Pontificalis, ed. Louis Duchesne, Paris, 1886–92.

Luther and Erasmus in *Library of Christian Classics* XVII, ed. E. G. Rupp *et al.*, on free will and determinism.

"Missale Gallicanum Vetus", ed. Jean Mabillon in *De Liturgia Gallicana*, 1685, reproduced in *PL* 72; edited again in *ALGC* and by L. C. Mohlberg, Rome, 1958. This edition contains the "Masses of Mone", in *PL* 138, cols 862–82 and in *ALGC*, but in a revised order which is reliable.

Missale Gothicum, ed. Mabillon in 1685, reproduced in *PL* 72, and edited again in *ALGC* and by H. M. Bannister for HBS, 1917–19.

St. Ambrose on the Sacraments and on the Mysteries, with E.T. by T. Thompson and introduction by J. H. Srawley, London, 1950; the same texts with French translation by Dom Bernard Botte, Paris, 1949.

Stowe Missal, ed. Б. MacCarthy in *Transactions of the Royal Irish Academy*, Dublin, 1886, and not so well by G. F. Warner for HBS, 1906–15.

Modern Books

Adam, Leonhard. *Primitive Art,* 3rd ed., London and Baltimore, 1954.

Bishop, Edmund. *Liturgica Historica,* Oxford, 1918.

Botte, Bernard. *Le canon de la messe romaine,* Louvain, 1935.

Bouyer, Louis. *Life and Liturgy,* London, 1956; published in U.S. as *Liturgical Piety,* Notre Dame, Ind., 1957.

——.*Rite and Man,* London and Notre Dame, Ind., 1963.

——.*Dom Lambert Beauduin, homme d'eglise,* Paris, 1964.

Brilioth, Yngve. *Eucharistic Faith and Practice, Evangelical and Catholic,* London and New York, 1930; revised ed. 1953.

Crichton, James D. *Christian Celebration: The Mass,* London, 1971, on the new *Missale Romanum* of 1970.

Cuming, Geoffrey J. *History of Anglican Liturgy,* London and New York, 1969.

Danielou, Jean. *The Bible and the Liturgy,* London and Notre Dame, Ind., 1956. E.T. of *Sacramentum Futuri,* Paris, 1950, on prophecy.

Dawson, Christopher. *The Age of the Gods,* London, 1928, London and New York 1937, on prehistory.

——.*Religion and Culture,* London and New York, 1948.

Douglas, Mary. *Natural Symbols,* London and New York, 1970.

Eliade, Mircea. *Patterns in Comparative Religion,* London and New York, 1958.

Every, George. *Basic Liturgy* (translations of eucharistic prayers), London, 1961.

Jungmann, Joseph. *The Mass of the Roman Rite,* London and New York, 2 vols with notes, 1952 and 1955; 1 vol. with more on consecration "by contact", 1959.

Klauser, Theodore. *The Western Liturgy and Its History,* London and New York, 1952.

Maringer, J. and Bandi, H. G. *Art in the Ice Age,* London and New York, 1953.

Martimount, A. G. *L'Eglise en prière; Introduction à la Liturgie.* 3rd ed. 1965, Paris and Tournai.

Martimont, A. G. (English Edition.) *The Church at Prayer.* Ed. by Flannery, Austin, O. P., and Ryan, Vincent, O.S.B.
Vol.I; *Introduction to the Liturgy.* Shannon, Ireland, 1968.
Vol. II; *The Eucharist.* Shannon, Ireland, 1973.

Masure, E. *The Christian Sacrifice,* London and New York, 1948.

Schillebeeckxe, E. *The Eucharist,* London and New York, 1968, on transubstantiation and sacrifice at the Council of Trent.

Sheppard, Lancelot. ed. *The New Liturgy,* London, 1970. Essays on the Missal.

Turner, Victor W. *The Ritual Process,* London and Chicago, 1969: London and Baltimore, Md., paperback, 1974.

Articles

In *Dictionnaire d'archéologie chrétienne et de liturgie,* ed. F. Cabrol and H. Leclerq, 1907–52, especially: "Liturgies Neo-Gallicanes" in IX, 1.

In *Dictionnaire de théologie catholique,* Paris, 1900–50: "Eucharistie" in V, especially J. de Ghellinck on the twelfth century, including the origin of the term transubstantiation; *Nil l'ascète* in XI, by M. T. Disdier, with reference to the Byzantine novelist who is not St. Nilus of Ancyra.

In *Concilium* II, 1 (February 1965): Hendrik Manders on Concelebration.

In *Maison-Dieu,* 103 (Paris, 1970): Pierre Journel on "Le missel de Paul VI", with special reference to the proper parts.

In *Year Book of Liturgical Studies,* Vol. 6, Collegeville, Minn., 1965: Paul Tihon on "Eucharistic Concelebration".

Acknowledgements

Many friends, dead and alive, have contributed to the line of thought developed in this book. The author would wish to thank the Rector of Oscott, Mgr Francis Thomas, Fr J. D. Crichton and Archimandrite Kallistos Ware for criticisms of particular chapters. They must not be reckoned responsible for the result.

Illustration credits

A.C.L. Bruxelles: 101, 107; Arch. phot. Paris: 150–151; Australian News Information Bureau: 18–19; Bibliothèque Nationale de Paris: 93, 96; W. Braun, Jerusalem: 46; British Library, The: 43, 44, 90, 103, 106; British Museum, The: 20, 23; Ciric, Geneva: 165, 183, 188–9, 192; City Art Gallery, Bristol: 41; City Art Gallery, Manchester: 32; Collection Musée de l'Homme, Paris: 15; Deutsche Fotothek, Dresden: 117(b); Dildarchiv Foto, Marburg: 159; Fotomas Index: 113(b), 125; Foto Stedelijk Museum, Amsterdam: 115; Franks, M. M.: 23; Gemeente Musea Van Amsterdam: 117(t); Keystone Press Agency Ltd.: 191; Kunsthistorichen Museums, Burgring: 37, 120; Kunstinstituts, Frankfurt: 33; Kupferstich Kabinett, Staatliche Museen Preussicher Kulturbesitz, W. Berlin: 111; Mansell Collection, The: 8, 9, 12, 16, 29, 35, 40, 48, 49, 50, 56, 58, 67, 68, 69, 75, 78–79, 81, 83, 85, 86, 87, 99, 105, 109, 113(t), 114, 116, 127; Mary Evans Picture Library: 97; National Monuments Record, Britain: 148; Oscott College: 39, 72, 73, 78, 122, 131, 132 t,b., 133, 134, 143, 146, 147 t,b., 152, 154; Radio Times Hulton Picture Library: 121, 135, 152, 153, 154; Rex Features Ltd: 27; Rosengarten Museums, Konstanz: 123; Sheridan, Ronald: 59, 63, 65; John Topham Picture Library: 175, 179; United Press International (UK) Ltd: 170–171; U.S.P.G.: 163, 167; Victoria & Albert Museum: 71; Yale University Art Gallery: 55.

Index